A Wife

on the

Alternative Pennine Way

by

Elizabeth R. Gregson

V·O·L·C·A·N·O
PUBLISHING

Volcano Publishing,
13 Little Lunnon,
Dunton Bassett,
Leics. LE17 5JR

© Elizabeth R. Gregson 1993

First published 1993
Revised and reprinted 1994

Typeset in 11 pt Bookman

Printed and bound in England

ISBN 1 898884 00 5

The 'alternative snails!' – designed by Ruth Gregson

Flower Illustrations by Rachel Smith

Other drawings by

Katharine Gregson

Flower Illustrations

Preface

From the comments which have been made since publication in 1993, it is obvious that readers have enjoyed my thoughts, as a wife, not just as a walking companion as is so often the case with books about long distance walking.

As I thought, this is a path yet to be discovered by many long distance walkers. However, I must stress again the need to be adequately equipped for some of the roughest terrain in the U.K. What starts off as a pleasant meander along the Tissington Trail from Ashbourne evetually becomes a real test of stamina over the northern moors where the weather can change so very quickly.

By way of compensation, Mr. Freeman in Coverdale (see introduction), is now open all day and sells this book in his shop. I am far to modest to suggest that this has anything to do with his staying open longer!

Elizabeth Gregson,
Leicester, 1994

Introduction

It may sound incredible but walking 275 miles in three weeks was actually the most relaxing holiday we have ever had. The worst part was having to come home again.

The Alternative Pennine Way was invented by *Denis Brook* and *Phil Hinchliffe,* both from my own home town of Huddersfield. Their guide was published by Cicerone Press in 1992 and we did the walk the following year. We only met two other people doing the same walk and they were together (although we have been told of others doing it).

The walk is excellent and so is the guidebook. Don't, however, be tempted to set off on the walk without also obtaining Ordnance Survey maps of the entire route. Study them well before setting out, especially the difficult parts where there is no visible path, such as on the way to Carlton. Nor should you ever go without a compass.

I would disagree with Messrs. Brook and Hinchliffe on one point. It *is* possible to buy provisions at Carlton-in-Coverdale. We found the Post Office-cum-Village Stores-cum-Tea Rooms to be very well stocked and the people very friendly, so much so that a month later we drove all the way there from Leicester for morning coffee and hot, buttered teacakes. To our dismay we were told by Mr. Freeman that in 1994 he may well have to close his shop in the afternoons as he only has six regular customers. I find it very sad to see small local shops being put out of business by superstores in nearby local towns.

So even if you don't fancy walking to Scotland, you may like to drive to Coverdale one morning!

As my publisher often tells me, anyone can write a book. I find that much the hardest part is to turn the manuscript into what you are now holding in your hands. For that my thanks go to Rachel, Katharine and Ruth for their delightful drawings, to Volcano Publishing for their professional expertise, and of course, to my wonderful husband for planning our walk and for encouraging me along the way.

Elizabeth Gregson,
Leicester, 1993

Our Route

JEDBURGH

Byrness

Bellingham

Haltwhistle

Allendale Town

Garrigill

Dufton

Kirkby Stephen

Hawes

Carlton-in-Coverdale

Pateley Bridge

Ilkley

Haworth

Hebden Bridge

Marsden

Dunford Bridge

Hathersage

Youlgreave

ASHBOURNE

Monday 19th July – Ashbourne

"We must be mad," said David as we climbed the hill out of Ashbourne. "Two hundred and seventy miles to go! If we'd stayed on that train we could have been in Jedburgh by this evening without having to pay for all the bed and breakfasts."

But this was what our holiday was all about: long distance walking with a comfortable bed at the end of every long day. We had done the Pennine Way in sections a couple of years ago and now we were hoping to do the Alternative Pennine Way all in one go.

People in Ashbourne are friendly. If we lived further away it would have been nice to have spent a night here before starting the walk but as it was, having considered various transport possibilities, we had been able to arrive at 10 a.m. after a very early start.

The first couple of miles were along the Tissington Trail, a former railway line out of Ashbourne. This is a much gentler initiation than the steep climb out of Edale on the original Pennine Way. We strolled along between banks of wild flowers, overtaken every now and then by cyclists who had hired their bikes in Ashbourne for an hour or two. We did wish that the bikes had been fitted with bells to warn us of their approach which often took us completely by surprise.

I had been wondering, during the last few weeks as I watched the Blue Meadow Crane's-bill coming into flower, whether it would still be in bloom by the time we began our holiday but here it was, all along the sides of the former track. After leaving this, some road and field walking took us to Thorpe

1

Cloud at the entrance to Dove Dale. Apparently the name "Cloud" simply means "hill" but it often seems an appropiate name to me. Coming round its eastern slopes was a pleasant experience for the grass was close-cropped and sprigged with flowers. I felt that I was in Switzerland. Then we came to a stream where flowers were growing that I had never seen before. When I first saw the leaves I wondered whether it was watercress but the bright yellow and red flowers, which had spread all the way down the stream, turned out to be Monkey flowers.

We came down to the stepping stones, paused to put on our waterproof trousers and followed the path up Dove Dale. Here the beautiful wooded slopes and interesting limestone rocks usually attract a lot of visitors but this Monday morning was fairly quiet. The River Dove continues up through Milldale (where we ate our sandwiches) and Wolfscote Dale but we turned right to go through the dry valley of Biggin Dale. Just beyond the village at Biggin we saw a notice advertising teas at a tiny little shop. Although the authors of "The Alternative Pennine Way" suggest that we should have been in Biggin by lunchtime, we don't believe in "flogging ourselves" so it was now well into the afternoon and we were ready for a cup of tea. We rang the bell and a lady came across the garden to direct us out of the drizzle into a summer-house where we revelled in the luxury of comfortable armchairs.

Before very long we joined another disused railway line, the High Peak Trail, which again made for easy walking for a short while. When we left the trail we had a most impressive view of the Minninglow Embankment and admired the skill of the Victorian engineers and navvies who built the railway.

Gratton Dale is another "dry valley" but this simply means that there is no stream to take away surplus water. Instead, after a few days of rain such as we had just had, it collects on the path which thereby becomes slippery with mud and our progress was considerably slowed down.

After a few days of rain, the path becomes slippery

We really should have taken notice of what the book said about the path beyond Dale End being "very wet in places". Then we could have taken the short cut to Youlgreave and kept our feet dry. As it was, we dutifully followed the instructions to turn off the road. If you can imagine an emerald green foam rubber mattress floating in a bath of water, you will know the sort of ground we were crossing. Every time we put our feet down, they were submerged to the ankles. We began to wonder why we were doing this walk. I began to think that sixteen and a half miles was far enough to have carried our evening meal.

Thankfully we came at last to a dry lane and were able to sit on the wall to eat our supper. All the cows in the field came to have a look. I felt as though we were at the Court of Versailles with all the courtiers watching the king and queen dine. One young bullock, obviously the Court Jester, decided to eat his way through the orange twine that was holding the gate up.

"Look out, number 179!" said David, as the animal began to lick the barbed wire. "You'd better be careful or you might end up in..." and I wondered whether he was going to say "oxtail stew" or "ham and tongue salad". He finished his sentence: :"You might end up in a book".

We had been down Bradford Dale before but I had never realised that the shallow, weedy areas in the river are actually disused cress beds. We climbed wearily up into Youlgreave and found the Old Bakery where Ann Croasdell gave us a warm welcome and did her best to dry our sodden footwear.

"Look out, number 179!", said David as the bullock began to lick the barbed wire

Tuesday 20th July – Youlgreave

We enjoyed breakfasting below the bread ovens in the Old Bakery, along with a couple from Essex who were getting to know the Peak District quite well during their stay in Youlgreave.

We walked out of the village in the other direction and down to the River Lathkill where I saw more Monkey-flowers growing in the trout ponds. As we climbed up through the woods on the other side of the valley I noticed Red Campion growing among the brambles. Through muddy cowfields and breezy sheep pastures we came to some open upland before descending to cross the River Wye. On our way down we had a good view of Haddon Hall, where William Peveril lived at the time of the Domesday Book, and we felt we must come back one day to visit the house.

For today, however, as we were combining two stages of the walk, we contented ourselves with skirting the grounds, The Great Willowherb, Meadowsweet, Wild Comfrey and Nettles were all more or less up to shoulder-height so I was glad that I was still wearing my protective clothing. The path was quite wet underfoot and would not be easy to negotiate in trainers. We passed between a field of barley and a hedge of docks and when we came to a road I found Meadow Vetchling growing on the verge. A pleasant climb up a wooded hillside brought us from the estate of the Duke of Rutland to that of the Duke of Devonshire.

I would never describe myself as a "nature lover". I am fascinated by the beauty of wild flowers and I love being in open country but I absolutely detest

*MEADOW VETCHLING has golden yellow flowers
very similar to those of Birdsfoot Trefoil.
This plant, however is taller. Its tendrils curl round the
stems of stronger plants to support it.*

having swarms of flies buzzing round my head. The walk through Manners Wood was beautiful and the path was clear and easy but when David put up the hood of his kagoule, it was immediately crawling with flies. I don't know what makes us so attractive to them: the colour? the heat? the smell? I am sure God had His reasons for creating flies. I can think of at least two: to pollinate flowers and to provide food for birds and spiders; but being neither a spider nor a flower myself, I find it hard to appreciate them. What I really *did* appreciate was the sense of relief and thankfulness when we came out of the woods and the breeze blew them away.

We ate our sandwiches in Chatsworth Park with a lovely view of the House and then walked on into Baslow. Time is allowed in the Alternative Pennine Way Guide for visiting Chatsworth House as well as Haddon Hall but we shall reserve those pleasures for a day in the future.

It is quite a toilsome climb up to Baslow Edge after having stiffened up in a tea-shop and before long, half of our party of two was straggling way behind the leader. Eventually however he sat down on a rock at the top to wait for me so at last I was able to drink the extra cup of tea which I had painstakingly carried up the hill. Polystyrene is a wonderful substance: the tea was still hot.

There is a broad, sandy track with outcrops of gritstone all the way along the escarpment so the going was easy. I had that wonderful feeling of our being all alone in the world, apart from a couple of cars in the distance, when I was startled by a loud noise and turned to see a large horse splashing through a puddle just behind me, Later on the same thing happened when we were overtaken by a boy on a bicycle with his dog. Mostly, however, there was a feeling of remoteness and tranquillity. The weather was perfect. The sun only broke through the clouds occasionally so it was not too hot and there is always a breeze up there on the top but there was no rain and very few puddles. From Curbar Edge we could see Cliff College. I remember going there to hear David Watson. He was explaining that if the greatest commandment is to love God with all our heart, then the greatest sin must be neither murder nor theft but *not* to love God with all my heart.

As we walked along Froggatt Edge, admiring the spectacular views, we were talking about common grace, the kindness of God that we haven't done anything to deserve and which is given freely to everybody, even to people who refuse to acknowledge that He exists.

The sense of openness started to evaporate as trees began to hem us in and the view down to our left disappeared. Then we walked along the road past the Grouse Inn for a little while. The blue Meadow Crane's-bill which I hadn't seen for a long time was there to cheer me on until we were able to leave the road.

We were no longer *on* an edge but we were *at* the edge of a wood. "Longshaw" apparently means "long copse" and it is a delightful place with plenty of space between the trees to our left so that we could easily see over towards Hathersage. After passing the beautiful Longshaw Lodge, which seemed to be peopled with cross-country runners, we stopped for tea and were accosted not by an athlete but by a large dog which must have been attracted by the smell of the food, until its master whistled it away.

We left the Alternative Pennine Way and walked down the main road into Hathersage. For a couple of miles we had magnificent views over the Derwent and Hope Valleys and the railway running along the bottom. The sun was low in the sky and the shadows emphasised the beauty of the landscape. There was a pavement to keep us safe from the traffic but I doubt whether many people walk that way because the lambs in the field to our left seemed terrified to see us. A little rabbit stared up at me with its big dark eyes for quite a long time before bounding off down the hill, almost knocking a sheep over in its headlong flight.

"Could you direct us to Ninelands Rd?" we asked a lady as we came into Hathersage.

"Would you by any chance be looking for Bankwood?" came the reply. It was Mrs. Rastall, bringing her son home from cubs. We admired their new pergola and then enjoyed cups of tea, a hot bath and a good night's sleep.

A little rabbit stared up at me with its big dark eyes.

Wednesday 21st July – Hathersage

Over breakfast we enjoyed a wide-ranging discussion with all three Rastall children, covering such topics as horticulture, geography and music. There was not much time, however, to sit and digest because we had to set off on our 20 mile walk. By 9-15 a.m. we were passing Hathersage Church where Little John is buried and then up we went past North Lees Hall where Jane Eyre stayed in Charlotte Brontë's novel.

Up Jacob's Ladder we were following in the footsteps of generations of stone cutters who walked up here to their work of shaping millstones. Despite the cloudy sky, the views were magnificent. I felt that I was looking down on Win Hill, Lose Hill and the Great Ridge leading along to Mam Tor although we were probably about on a level with them. From the trig point we could see over to Sheffield on our right. All the way we had the wind in our hair and the choice of putting our feet on millstone grit or springy turf, with only the occasional patch of boggy peat.

The sun was shining on me as I went to sleep in the heather for ten minutes before the stony track led us down to join the road at Moscar. We soon turned off in the direction of the Strines Inn. A beautiful sign dated 1935 indicated the path to Derwent Edge. It was boggy but there were buttercups and tormentil among the reeds and rushes. We came to another sign: 1933 this time and its arrowhead had fallen off but we guessed *right!*

There was some brilliant sunshine during our ascent among the shooting butts but enough wind to prevent the strenuous climb from making us feel

We discussed topics such as horticulture.

I have always loved the dainty little TORMENTIL,
its four-petalled yellow flowers,
each on its own, tiny stalk.

14

too hot and sticky. The path led us clearly up to where we turned right along Derwent Edge with a superb view down over Derwent Reservoir. Surrounded by dark conifers, its waters were bravely trying to reflect the clear blue sky.

As we approached the very impressive pile of rocks known variously as the Wheelstones or the Coach and Horses, I reflected that I would rather be on my own two feet than in any wheeled vehicle on such a stony, rock-strewn path. Beyond the Wheelstones it occurred to me that if the Alternative Pennine Way becomes more popular, somebody will have to start working on erosion control of the footpaths. Then, beyond the next rock formation (the Cakes of Bread), there was ample evidence that the National Trust is already doing just that. Not only was it more pleasant to put my feet on to slabs of solid rock than into boggy peat but I had no need to feel guilty about making life more difficult for some poor bilberry plant or tussock of grass, already having a struggle to survive in such an exposed place.

We turned right and headed down to find a sheltered spot to eat the sandwiches that Mrs. Rastall had packed for us. We were still quite high up and although the heather was comfortable, and the sun shone bravely, the wind was still cold and my fingers went numb as I ate my crisps. The way was downhill, however, and by the time we reached Howden Reservoir I was too hot in my kagoule. We had hoped to cross the dam and go to the car park on the other side where we knew there would be a toilet but the dam gates were closed. Never mind, the waterworks road, despite its mud and puddles,

"I'm giving up!"

provided for easy walking and we were able to pray together as we went along.

Beyond Slippery Stones Bridge we came to a fork. "Foot-path" it said to the left and "Bridleway" to the right. The footpath looked more promising but our route took us along the bridleway. Before long we saw a man climbing down the hill, bearing aloft a bicycle in one hand "That looks heavy," I said as we met him. He put down his bike.

"I'll tell you what," he said, "if that track's rideable..." and he paused to consider, "I'm giving up!" With that, he picked up his bike and carried on down the hill.

He was quite right. The path was narrow and scrambling, up a stony slope so steep as to be almost vertical in places. But it led us into a beautiful, remote valley.

"Now this," I said to myself, "this is *real* Pennine country."

Up at the top of Howden Edge we sat down for a biscuit and to admire the magnificent view. We could see Win Lose Hill, Mam Tor, Kinder and even the Hope Cement Factory in this beautiful sweep of Pennine terrain, round from Margery Hill to our left.

We turned our backs on all that because we still had a long way to go. Gradually we climbed to Cut Gate, then on over Featherbed Moss and along Mickleden Edge. We were thankful to have such a good day for this stage of the Alternative Pennine Way . What could have been an ordeal became instead an intensely pleasurable experience. The path was clearly defined and the late afternoon sun was lighting up the wonderful emptiness of the moors. There was one man making his lonely way up towards us.

"Are you going all the way over tonight?" I asked when we finally met.

"Well, there are still four hours of daylight left," he replied.

It was true that in that isolated place there was a sense of timelessness. I felt as though I could have gone on walking there forever and this must indeed have been one of the best sections of the whole walk.

All good things come to an end, however; at least, in this world they do. We came down to cross the Little Don River and then there were trees and woods and roads and lanes: all things that are good and useful in their place but which had been gloriously absent for most of the afternoon.

The Stanhope Arms at Dunford Bridge does offer accommodation but a dear friend of ours in Huddersfield had agreed to pick us up. Christine provided not only warm hospitality but also a delicious vegetarian meal.

*It isn't easy fitting two large rucksacks
into the boot of a small car.*

19

Thursday 22nd July – Dunford Bridge

Oh! what a beautiful morning it was as we set out past Winscar and Harden reservoirs. The sun was shining on the water and a Longley Farm lorry trundled past us as we walked up the road. We negotiated the stone quarries but couldn't find the track across the moor so had to make our own way through clumps of heather and tussocks of grass. This was the sort of walking where each step is as high as it is long.

As we came down from Hades Farm a cloud of flies rose from a cow-pat at our approach and appeared to have every intention of escorting us for the rest of our journey.

Having left my heavy rucksack in Huddersfield for the day, I eventually succeeded in running faster than they could fly but whenever I stopped to gather a bilberry they threatened to catch up with me again and I had to pick a frond of bracken to use as a fly-swat. Meanwhile my brave husband strode manfully on behind, using the hood of his kagoule to distract the flies from his wife-in-distress.

We found ourselves looking down into the Holme Valley. How tidy and civilised it looked in the sunshine. Castle Hill certainly looked more imposing from here than it had done yesterday from Mickleden Edge. A bank of wild flowers intrigued me. I couldn't identify the tiny white, four-petalled flowers and the neat little rosettes of spiky leaves. In fact it was another six days before I found out what they were.

We crossed the dam between Riding Wood and Ramsden Reservoirs in glorious sunshine. I want to stress this fact for the sake of any foreigners who may be still under the misapprehension that the sun never shines in the North of England. On our way up again we missed the path and for the second time that day had to cross a stretch of uneven ground where we were knee-deep in tussocky grass I find this sort of walking more exhausting than climbing a mountain.

There are several plants which have small, white flowers with four petals. One is the sweet-smelling Woodruff, another is Goosegrass with its pairs of hooked seeds and a third is HEATH BEDSTRAW

At the top we decided to stop to eat our sandwiches where we had a good view down the Holme Valley. As it was our Wedding Anniversary, it was appropriate that I was reading a book about the five types of love that are essential for building a successful marriage: sexual attraction, romantic love, loyal commitment, mutual sharing and the sacrificial love that the Lord Jesus Christ demonstrated in His life and death. Even after twenty-six years it is good to be challenged to make our marriage better still.

We clambered down to the stream and up into the village of Holme then up again to Stopes Moor on an easy track which we knew well. This time, however, because there was no need to retrace our steps to collect the car, we were able to carry on down into beautiful Marsden Clough, whose stream flows into Digley Reservoir, before climbing up to Bradshaw and another familiar path. On the way across the fields I found that little white flower again, a smaller variety this time.

We came up to Wessenden Head and crossed what I have always known as the Isle of Skye road, although the inn of that name disappeared many years ago. Again we could see those two landmarks overlooking Huddersfield: the VHF Radio transmitter at Holme Moss and the concrete mast at Emley Moor. I thought back to a year or two after we were married, one freezing cold evening when all those people in the North of England who were watching ITV suddenly saw their screens go blank and jumped up to switch channels, wondering what had happened their television set. There on BBC was a newsreader gleefully announcing that the ITV mast at Emley Moor had collapsed under the weight of the ice which had accumulated on it.

We had often walked down the Wessenden Valley, ever since my sister and I were quite small and our parents wondered whether they might end up having to carry us. It was particularly appropriate for David and me to be coming down it today because that was where we first fell in love, one rainy day in winter. Today was, however, the first time we had ever used the high level path which follows the course of the conduit.

It was a day for "ruin-hunting" as someone once described the nostalgic hobby of revisiting old haunts. "There's the wall where we sheltered from the rain". "Down there is where we had a picnic when we were getting the house ready." "This is where we brought your cousins." "Isn't that the house where our friends used to live?"

We came into Marsden down the steps beside the reservoir embankment, again something I had never done when we lived there. I counted them silently-209... 210...211. It was good to be in Marsden again and to see all the places we remembered but we didn't see anyone we recognised and hadn't time to call because we were off to my parents' for an anniversary dinner.

Friday 23rd July – Marsden

Climbing up from Spring Head Lane we realised that we were seeing parts of Marsden that we had never visited in all the years we lived here. On a muddy stretch I missed my footing and my shriek of horror woke the sleeping dogs, who barked in chorus while we were negotiating the gate and stile. The little dog squeezed his way out and jumped up and down in excitement.

We headed in the direction of Pole Moor along a squelchy path. It was simpler walking on the remains of a dry-stone wall where it was easy to see the "throughs", the long stones which go the whole width of the wall to tie it together.

Our route diverged from that of the Colne Valley Circular Walk and we came to the small Cupwith Reservoir. A couple of dozen ducks jumped into the water, startled. A dry cinder path led us to the Nont Sarah's road. (All the roads out of Huddersfield seem to be identified by their public houses!) We looked back to admire the view over Deer Hill Reservoir and tried to pick out the Wessenden Valley where we were walking yesterday.

Crossing the road, we passed a solitary farmhouse and came down a path which I could only describe as 'mucky' to Deanhead Reservoir. Scrambling up the other side I noticed more of those anonymous little white flowers growing in the grass and then at last, having crossed the Brown Cow road, we sat down in the grass for a breather.

We had already passed Scammonden Water and seen all the motorway traffic speeding across the dam. Now here below us was the M62, the 'Motorway across the Pennines', at the point where the two carriage ways separate to form a little island. I felt very proud of the Yorkshire farmer who insisted that his farm remain intact, despite being right where the motorway was planned to run. Now we were going to cross under it, using the tunnels that constitute the drive to his front door. To our left we could see the footbridge where the Pennine Way crosses over it and I felt rather envious of walkers using that high-level route as I considered the ups and the downs that we were going to have to negotiate.

We came down towards the tidy farmhouse and I supposed that its inhabitants must soon get used to the constant drone of traffic. As we came nearer to the subways I found myself wondering whether they were not too fragile to support such a huge volume of traffic and to stop an articulated lorry from falling on my head. Underneath them there was plenty of room, which was being utilised as extra storage space.

I pondered the question of motorways. If I have the choice, I always prefer to use them because they make the journey smoother and faster; and yet I am not happy about the rate at which the Department of Transport is seeking to extend the existing network. Am I being irrational? No, I decided, I'm not. It's simply a question of moderation. I like cream cakes but too many make me ill. Similarly, an occasional glass of wine may be pleasant but the excessive consumption of alcohol can be dangerous. In the same way, a limited number of motorways can be useful but there are probably enough of them by now and the enviromental aspect needs to be considered very carefully before any more link roads or by-passes are built.

We had come into Calderdale now and were looking up at the enormous dam of Booth Wood Reservoir. We had to walk up the Oldham to Ripponden road for a little way and I counted Thistles, Ragwort, Oxeye daisies, Yarrow, Clover, Cat's-ear and Bird's-foot-trefoil along the roadside. Unfortunately, that wasn't all. I also saw cigarette packets, lager cans, peanut bags, plastic cups and even milk bottles. I confess that I didn't stop to pick them up, thinking that I already had enough to carry with my rucksack.

Rishworth Lodge restaurant must have been a very attractive venue for wedding receptions before it was closed. We climbed up beyond it to open moorland where we sat down to eat our sandwiches, sheltering as best we could behind a wall from the freezing cold wind. After that we were in farmland. A sheep and her lamb were walking towards a "creeple hole" in the drystone wall. The lamb got there first but I could almost hear the mother sheep saying, "Stand back for your elders" as she pushed him out of the way and squeezed through first. At the farm, children were running into doorways to shelter from the rain and as we crossed Baitlings Dam we watched a raincloud gusting across the reservoir and down the valley. Country lanes make for easier walking but (in our case at least) can make navigation more difficult. We put on two extra miles before thankfully recognising the turning to the Calderdale Way which we had walked last Easter.

Whereas a Daisy's leaves are compact and hairy and those of the Scentless Mayweed are hair-like, the OXEYE DAISY has feathery leaves.

CAT'S-EAR has flowers and leaves
quite similar to those of a Dandelion but nits stalk is not
hollow and bears small bracts, shaped like cat's ears.

We followed it down to Cragg Vale and were surprised to see that the undertaker's car was not parked where it always has been when we have passed before.

Just as we had seen, on the Brown Cow road this morning, our first ever 'APW' sign, so now we came to the first of those flagged paths which are so typical of Calderdale. It always sets my imagination going, thinking of the generations of Yorkshire men and women who have trudged up and down these paths. Although this particular one is on both the Calderdale Way and the Alternative Pennine Way, it was somewhat overgrown, making me wonder how many people take advantage of these long distance walks.

The Hinchliffe Arms in Cragg Vale is the only place where we could have hoped to find a cup of tea but we had to make do with coffee and lemonade. By the time we came out, the rain had stopped.

We had never seen the beautiful Cragg Old Hall before. We should have walked right past it but we took another wrong turning and a kind local resident had to come out of his cottage to show us how to rejoin the A.P.W. without getting too muddy. Really, he needn't have bothered because the flagged path we found on Bell House Moor after half a mile or so went three inches under water. The moorland on either side was even worse. In such conditions I find that it actually becomes easier to walk because once your socks and boots are soaking wet, there is no point in trying to keep them dry, so you just plod on, regardless of whether you are on dry grass or in a swamp. In that way we were able at last to join a track which took us directly (and almost vertically) down into Hebden Bridge.

Although I have heard the A.P.W. described as a "geriatric version of the Pennine Way", I should recommend that anyone over eighty intending to walk it should first test themselves out on this short section from Cragg Vale to Hebden Bridge (about 3 miles) and allow themselves all day to do it in, especially if they choose to do it one week after a wet St. Swithen's Day, as we did. We were glad to know from past experience that Mrs. Morley would have hot water and dry towels waiting for us at Slack Top.

First, however, we stopped in Hebden Bridge for something to eat. There was a bewildering choice of cafés, fish and chip shops, Indian curry houses and Chinese takeaways. In the end we chose to buy something in a supermarket and eat it on a public bench. The trouble was that we both felt tempted by the tubs of coleslaw but we couldn't find any spoons. The only solution was to use potato crisps!

INDIAN BALSAM
With its large pink flowers, is so impressive that at first
I thought it had escaped from somebody's garden.
In fact it was introduced to this country
from the Himalayas.

Saturday 24th July – Hebden Bridge

We said Goodbye to the Morleys and walked back down from Slack Top into Heptonstall with its cobbled streets of weavers' cottages. In a shop window I noticed books about the Cragg Vale Coiners. The "King" of them, David Hartley, whose farm on Bell House Moor we had passed yesterday, was buried in Heptonstall Churchyard after being executed for the murder of an excise man. I hoped that the poor officer had at least been able to keep his feet dry as he trudged up from Cragg Vale to meet his death. At any rate his murderers were punished for setting financial gain above the value of a man's life. I thought back to the Great Train Robbery...

We left Heptonstall along Northgate, past the round Methodist Church, and headed down through steep woods to cross Hebden Water at Midge Hole. This time we didn't catch sight of the woodpecker we had seen on this section of the Calderdale Way. We did, however, meét a family coming up who rather surprised us because the little girl was holding aloft a pretty, pink umbrella, even though the morning was fine and dry.

"It's as well to be prepared, though, isn't it!" commented her father.

In Crimsworth Dean there were a lot of handsome, pink flowers which I discovered are called Indian Balsam and some less conspicuous, greenish yellow Wood Sage. The trees are deciduous and very attractive but still it was good to be out of them and climbing into the upper reaches of the valley towards open moorland.

"It's as well to be prepared!"

The drystone walls enclosing the fields were large-
ly in a poor state of repair and the sheep and cattle
seemed to be free to roam with only an occasional
strand of barbed wire to control them. We passed a
lovely old stone farmhouse with three storeys of
mullioned windows but it was abandoned and roofless. Through a window with no glass we could see
an old stone fireplace I hoped that somebody would
come along and renovate the building before it got
any worse.

We stopped for a rest. David cast down his rucksack with rather too much abandon...and then had
to run after it as it rolled down the hillside gathering momentum. We were reminded of a friend
whose holiday in Scotland was abruptly curtailed
when he lost his rucksack and never managed to
retrieve it.

As we walked on again we noticed a man scything
thistles in a field ahead and further on we saw a
field of windmills on a hilltop to our right. When we
sat down to eat our sandwiches, our view over to
Haworth was dominated by another windmill, its
three sails spinning madly in the wind. Clearly,
Yorkshire is becoming a land of environmental
enthusiasts.

Two girls on horseback reined in and waited
politely for us to pass. We were descending Bodkin
Lane, which is very steep but not frighteningly so
because it is so stony. I tried to decide whether the
stones were natural or whether they had been set in
place manually. I could hardly believe that they had
because the lane was extremely wide and didn't
really lead anywhere. Further down, the stones had

been covered with tarmac in uneven patches and here I really did have to watch where I put my feet. It set me' thinking about how God is described in the Bible as a rock and is completely trustworthy, whereas man-made religions and philosophies are dangerous and unreliable.

As we came down through Penistone Hill Country Park, I thought, "Yes, I'm glad so many people come to Haworth. I'm glad there are all these little paths and sign-posts and car parks and even a public toilet, to attract people up on to the moors. I'm glad to see two whole families busily gathering bilberries: it reminds me of how much I enjoyed doing exactly the same when I was a child. But, "I thought", the moors here, overlooking the Worth Valley, with all the farms and hamlets on the other side of the river, these moors are not a patch on the moors we've been walking across: Stairs Hill where we've just had lunch, Rishworth Moor, Wessenden Moor, Howden Moor, even the sogginess of Bell House Moor last night. I'm glad we're doing the Alternative Pennine Way."

We were walking along a flagged path and suddenly realised that Haworth Parish Church was in front, the grave yard on our left and the Brontë Parsonage beyond. We turned a corner and the peace and quiet were shattered as we stepped down into Main Street where there is all the bustle of a Tourist Centre. There were tea rooms, craft shops, bookshops and, down the cobbled street and beyond the park, the station with its steam trains on the Keighley and Worth Valley Railway.

Sunday 25th July – Haworth.

We had planned our holiday so that Sunday should be a rest day and where better to rest than at Hole Farm which Mr. and Mrs. Milner have restored so impressively. We were provided with all we could ever need, from shampoo to wild boar sausages, from a bowl of fruit to a carriage clock, and we had a really relaxing day.

Twice we walked over the fields to Hall Green Baptist Church where we enjoyed warm fellowship and good teaching from Rev. Keith Dredge. He pointed out that in our land today most people take no notice of the church because it seems to have as much backbone as a jelly but that the Lord Jesus Christ had real authority and His followers should speak with the authority of God's Word.

Back at Hole Farm we met piglets, peacocks, bantams and calves, not forgetting Gilbert Turkey. We never saw Mrs. Turkey as she was sitting on eggs.

Monday 26th July – Haworth

Down at the Station the 78022 (standard 2-6-0) was already getting steam up for its first run of the day to Keighley. We were heading in the same direction, climbing first of all up to Brow Moor, and the windmill we had noticed on Saturday. It supplies the quarry with all the electricity it needs and the sale of surplus power will have paid the installation cost within four years.

At the Three Sisters restaurant we turned off the road on to a path along the hillside where a man was picking the best bilberries I have ever seen. As we walked along, David kept looking at his watch and keeping an eye on the K.W.V.R. line across the valley. At last we saw a puff of smoke and the steam train ambled by. Further along, a yellow steam engine painted on a gate post showed us that we were still on the route of the "Railway Children's" walk from Haworth Station and for the second time that morning I picked out a house which may or may not have been "Three Chimneys" in E. Nesbit's story.

We were coming down through some woods where Indian Balsam was growing, when I suddenly realised that Bingley was nearer than I had thought. Soon we were crossing under the Leeds, Settle & Carlisle Railway and walking up through some allotments to the three-rise locks which were festooned with Corydalis and backed by the Damart Mill.

We walked along the Leeds and Liverpool Canal to the five-rise staircase and sat on a wall to eat our sandwiches. It was quite a pleasant day, despite the

The first thing I ever learnt about BILBERRIES was
that they might make your teeth go purple.
It takes a long time to gather enough to make a pie
because they are so small.

occasional drizzle, and plenty of people were out for a stroll. A narrow boat was on its way down the staircase and there was no shortage of willing hands to help with the lock gates.

We walked along the towpath, past a drift of Blue Meadow Crane's bill and Meadowsweet. Two ladies, up in Bingley for the day, asked us how far we were going.

"We were just trying to decide whether to walk to Liverpool along the towpath", they told us.

We left the canal and went up, past a drift of Blue Scabious, to the pretty village of Micklethwaite. A tree and a seat commemorated the fact that Micklethwaite had twice been the winner of the best-kept village competition. For a short distance we followed the steep Keighley to Otley road, whose verges were silver with Mugwort.

Then we came to the part of the walk I had been waiting for all day. The path over Bingley Moor was what moorland paths used to be, before thousands of hikers (including ourselves, of course) came traipsing across the hills, eroding the vegetation. Perhaps we shouldn't be encouraging people to walk the A.P.W. after all!

I don't really like to see patches of moor where the heather has been burnt but when such as authority as David Bellamy says that the grouse could not survive without this periodic renewing of their habitat, I suppose we have to believe him. Certainly, in the parts where the heather had started growing again, it looked young, strong and healthy and the whole moor was carpeted with heather, whereas over the other side of Rombalds Moor (which is

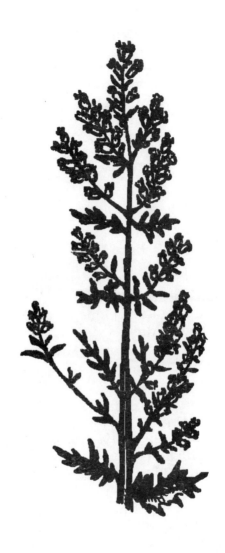

MUGWORT has small white flowers with reddish-brown centres but in July I found it easier to recognise the plant by its downy leaves which are silver on the back.

made up of fourteen different moors altogether), Ilkley Moor had less heather, more grass and a lot of bracken too.

As we climbed, we could see a panorama of Yorkshire towns and cities below and behind us: Leeds, Bradford, Keighley... with Pendle Hill away to the right and Emley Moor mast over in the distance where we had been four or five days ago.

David was wearing his cloth cap pulled well down on to his head, determined not to catch his death of cold but I defiantly walked over Ilkley Moor "baht 'at". We came to White Wells on the edge of the moor, where cold water bath cures were fashionable over two hundred years ago. I should have thought this would be much more likely to lead to catching one's death of cold.

I always have difficulty in keeping up with David, whether we are going up hills or coming down them. He kindly waits for me every now and then but this afternoon he seemed to be in a hurry and I suddenly guessed that he was wondering whether Betty's teashop would still be open. What a misinterpretation on my part! He was rushing to find a bookshop before they all closed.

Tuesday 27th July – Ilkley

We left the comforts of Hollygarth Guest House, where Mrs. Taylor's breakfast was excellent value for money, and walked back along Leeds Road to have another look at Ilkley's bookshops. On the way I noticed that the launderette closes at 8pm Mon-Fri. and 5pm at weekends. I called at The Lunchbox: apparently people travel from Scotland to buy their sandwiches there.

We came down to the River Wharfe and joined the Dales Way (73 miles to Bowness, whereas we still had 169 to do). We followed the river all the way to the pretty village of Addingham, passing a lot more Indian Balsam and the attractive Nettle-leaved Bellflower growing on the river banks.

We passed a field where a proud mother cow appeared to have just finished licking clean the newborn calf lying at her feet. From there the path was steep and slimy but in dry weather it would have been very pretty with all the pink flowers: Red Campion, Foxgloves, Herb Robert, Betony, Yarrow and Woundwort.

At Currer Hall I guessed that this must have been where Charlotte Brontë found her pseudonym of Currer Bell. We had to walk through fields where the long grass wet our socks and we wished we had been wearing gaiters, so after crossing the A59 we decided to stick to the little country road and to miss out Bolton

BELLFLOWER
is a tall plant with pink or mauve bell-shaped flowers.
It is related to the Companulas
that we find in the garden.

YARROW is a very common plant.
It even grows profusely in our lawn, although we don't
often allow its white flowers to appear there.
Its other name is "Millfoil" which means a thousand leaves,
because of its soft feathery leaves.

Abbey which we have visited many times before. (Its proper name is the Priory of St. Mary at Bolton). We understand that it is still being well looked-after by the Duke of Devonshire.

We passed a bank of Wood Sage, the plant I had first noticed in Crimsworth Dean near Hardcastle Crags and then, just above Storiths, David's attention was drawn to a sign with a steam engine on it. It said, "Back o' th' Hill Farm. Buffers Coffee Shop and Model Railway Gallery". We wondered whether or not to go in but as our boots were not too muddy now, we plucked up courage...and were so glad we did. It was a series of Aladdin's Caves opening off from each other and when I ordered a jacket potato it was served with an incredible variety of salad and fruit.

Walking along the banks of the Wharfe, we realised that we had gone past the bridge to Barden Tower without thinking to cross it. Never mind: there would probably not have been time to see more of the Tower than we have seen on previous occasions.

The Strid was very different. I have often heard about it and never really wanted to go. It sounds so frightening: the whole River Wharfe hurtling through a gap less than six feet wide. I was even more horrified to read in the A.P.W. guide that when people try to jump it and fall in, due to the under-water potholes, they may not come up for air for several days, by which time it is too late.

I did not exactly enjoy struggling along the rocky bank and was in no way tempted to jump from the slippery stones on one side to the moss-covered rocks on the other. Still it was quite an experience to gaze down at the churning waters beneath us.

The Wharfe then became much calmer and we walked between hayfields on our right and, to our left, the river bank, colourful with Scabious, Yarrow, Ragwort and Meadowsweet, to name but a few of the flowers growing there. I guessed that the farmers there harvest two crops of hay a year because the only flowers that had been able to seed themselves in the grass of the fields were Dandelions.

We left the river and turned up a side valley, still along country lanes. At a well equipped caravan site we bought a Mars bar, well aware that the only time you can eat Mars bars without the risk of putting on weight is just before some strenuous exercise, so that the sugar is used as energy, rather than being converted into fat. We still had several miles to walk, mostly uphill, so we felt safe.

We must have added at least an extra half-mile whilst trying to find the right gate through which to leave Howgill Lane. By the time we had found the footbridge and were halfway up to High Crag, I was needing another "breather". I remembered a verse that had been read out at a wedding we attended just before we set out: "Husbands, dwell with your wives according to knowledge". I cannot say how Peter, who wrote those words, treated his wife but I began to think that God who inspired him to write them, included in the meaning of "knowledge" the idea that men should recognise that women walk better if they are allowed short but frequent rests.

I had expected to be able to see Pateley Bridge

from the top but we obviously had a long way to go yet. This was another of these wonderfully remote and desolate areas. There were signs, however, that people had once worked here, mining lead and silver, and had even lived here. I tried to imagine what life would be like for them. There would be plenty of mutton and rabbit but would they be able to grow carrots and onions to put in their stews?

We came out on to the Grassington to Pateley Bridge Road and walked down it towards Greenhow. Here was my answer. Several farms appeared to have been recently modernised and in some cases had most attractive gardens. If flowers could grow up here, then so could vegetables.

We were still quite high up (around twelve hundred feet) and it was very cold. I was so glad not have taken any notice of my Second Cousin Christopher. He told me that cycle capes "went out with the ark" and that to wear mine would only invite jokes about the R.N.L.I.. I looked round and could see only sheep. Surely they hadn't heard very much about life-boats! Meanwhile, my cape was keeping me warm and dry so I was glad to be wearing it.

We ate our tea over-looking the quarries and appreciated the sandwiches with the international reputation. We watched a group of half-grown lambs butting each other. Was it a case of bullying? Or was it just their version of contact sports? At this distance it was hard to tell. What we could see was that in between rounds they all broke off to nibble furiously at the grass, as if to make up for wasted time.

As we came down the Nidderdale Way towards Patley Bridge, the wind grew less strong and the temperature rose appreciably once we were in the shelter of the valley. We began to wonder whether one of these outlying farms might be Fellbeck where we were spending the night. We carefully inspected every gatepost we came to but found ourselves right down in the town without finding it.

We asked a man who was just getting out of his ꞓar.

"Fellbeck?" he repeated, "What name is it? Nelsons? You've a fair way to go yet. It'll be another couple of miles from the bridge."

It was half past nine already so we thought we ought to phone. What a relief when Mr. Nelson offered to come and pick us up in his Land-Rover!

Wednesday 28th July – Pateley Bridge

We were a little worried that we might not be able to arrive in Coverdale in time for the evening meal so we phoned to cancel it. Then, as if in answer to prayer, a fellow guest offered us a lift down into Pateley Bridge. Maurice and his wife were staying at the Nelsons' for the fifth year running: that's some recommendation! They were hoping to visit Masham in Wensleydale that day and dropped us off in Pateley Bridge on the way.

We set off along the eastern bank of the River Nidd, walking on the track bed of the Nidd Valley Light Railway which closed in 1936. It had been used to transport men and materials when the reservoirs at the head of the dale were being built. As we walked along beside Gouthwaite reservoir we came to a huge, muddy puddle. The only way round it was to hang on for dear life to an iron railing that was leaning out towards us at an angle of 45°. For the most part, however, this section was very, very much easier than when we were walking alongside Haweswater Reservoir last year on the Coast to Coast.

The previous evening we had seen a rabbit that appeared to be blind. Now we saw another that seemed to have its eyes closed – only a young one this time. It ran away very quickly but it was zig-zagging all over the place.

At last we came to Bouthwaite, a pretty village at the head of the reservoir. The hedgerows were full of Woundwort and those little white flowers whose names I had not yet discovered. There were also those big teasel-like purple flowers which I had seen last year and finally a weed which I quickly recognised as Cleavers or Goosegrass draping itself

The big purple flower I finally discovered to be BURDOCK.

over the hawthorn hedges.

Ramsgill was another attractive village. We sat down on the village green for a rest. We didn't see the peacocks but watched people arriving at the hotel for morning coffee. That was some thing we didn't need after Mrs. Nelson's wonderful breakfast. Half a dozen white geese, in a field that we passed, stood motionless in a line, as though posing for a photo. Then one after another, they each in turn took one step forwards. I was glad that we were making faster progress!

After a stop for sandwiches we passed How Stean Gorge and came through the village of Lofthouse, where we stopped to buy some postcards in the village store and post office. As we walked along a farm track, I began wondering how I could attach a piece of fly paper to my rucksack. I remembered reading that the oil in an orange skin is lethal to flies. Perhaps we should be offered fresh grapefruit for breakfast and then I could concoct a fly trap out of the grapefruit skin.

We met a family who commented on all the dead rabbits they had seen, just as I had been thinking about the same subject. Apparently this is a bad year for Myxamatosis because there was not enough hard frost last winter to kill all the germs. This was obviously what was wrong with the little rabbit we had seen that morning. Nevertheless, I have read in a magazine article that the disease is now much weaker than it used to be and that rabbit populations are increasing rapidly.

At last we started to climb steeply away from the farmland with its flies and up to the skyline. To my

*I wondered whether I could concoct a fly trap
out of a grapefruit skin.*

mind, the worst thing about the A.P.W. is its variety! People have complained that the Pennine Way is monotonous but I personally find country lanes, woodland glades and village greens rather boring. Perhaps this is why I have developed an interest in wild flowers, to give me something to think about while we walk, Perhaps it is also why I write books!

Now, however, we were coming up to the moors and it was still only mid-afternoon. We had the sun on our faces and the wind in our hair. There were no flies and as we walked along Thrope Edge and Dale Edge we had a beautiful view, first of all down Nidderdale and later on along Upper Nidderdale towards Great Whernside.

We sat down to eat our dessert and rest under the clear blue sky, to gather our strength for the trek through the heather after leaving the track.

At this point, I think I should warn any readers who are considering doing the same walk, that if the sky had not been clear and blue and if we had not still had five hours of daylight in front of us, the next part of this walk could have been very dangerous. There is no path at all. The dotted lines on the map simply indicate rights of way.

Sometimes you walk through grass and sometimes heather or bilberries. The grass is the worst because it is tussocky, which makes balancing difficult. It goes against the grain with me to walk on bilberries but I soon realised that there were no berries visible and, if there had been, no one would be likely to come gathering them apart from the few sheep. These animals took one look and fled from us as though we were aliens.

The heather was the best for walking. It has so much spring in it that it didn't seem to suffer from our passage. I remember my aunt telling me that when she used to go camping (and that was before camping became the luxury activity it is today), the best place to put your sleeping bag was on a bed of heather. Sometimes we were doing what I think of as 'feather bed walking'. Your feet sink in and you are not quite sure what you are treading on. The easiest places were where the heather had been burnt and you could actually see the ground or where it was just starting to grow again and was quite low.

My great advantage is that I have a husband who is quite happy to walk in front so that it is he who stumbles into the little rivulets and drainage channels, which I can then avoid. This often reminds me of Hebrews chapter 2 where the Lord Jesus Christ is described as a "perfect leader" or the pioneer of our salvation. He has already gone through everything that we have to go through, including death.

First we identified one hill on the horizon and made our way up to it and then another hill on another horizon far away and walked towards that. The little bump on top turned out to be a gate in a fence and when we finally arrived at it we sat down in the sun to eat our apples. I felt as though I were on top of the world, although behind me Great Whernside was higher than we were.

This was where we made the mistake of forgetting to consult the compass again. We could see where we were heading for and went straight towards it. Unfortunately this meant that once we reached the bottom of the hill we had to make our way across a marsh. What with that and trying to find our way round walls and barbed wire, it was already late by the time we found ourselves in Swineside.

A signpost indicated the way to a bridge a mile away but soon the path divided, the other signpost was hidden and we took the wrong fork. We found ourselves at the river but although a tractor could have forded it, there was no bridge for us to use. We tried to rejoin the other path but barbed wire foiled our attempts and we had to climb back up the steep fields to where we had set out.

In the gathering dusk we followed the field path down to the river again, where beautiful Bellflowers blossomed near to the stone bridge. But where was Carlton? Another signpost indicated that it was still half a mile away across more fields. We were glad that the stiles were clearly marked but less happy when the official path went through a bog.

It was getting almost too dark to make out the next stile across a field but at last we came out on the main road through Carlton. Now the problem was to find Middleham House in this mile-long village but as Mrs. Allinson had told us she lived opposite the shop, we were able to enquire and soon were standing on her doorstep. She seemed amazed to see us as her husband had just gone out the other way in his Land-Rover to look for us.

She welcomed us into their beautiful home, an old cottage which he has restored, and put our boots to dry in her kitchen. We were thankful we had phoned that morning to cancel the evening meal as by now we were no longer hungry. It was quarter past ten.

Thursday 29th July – Carlton-in-Coverdale

We woke to the sound of the stream, gurgling outside our bedroom window. Drawing back the curtain, I found on the windowsill all I could have needed for washing up, had we been travelling by car with a picnic basket. After a copious breakfast we left Middleham House, bought some sandwiches at the well-stocked Post Office and walked to the end of the village to begin the climb out of Coverdale and over into Waldendale.

I prefer a start like this. Yesterday we had meandered around in Nidderdale for eight or nine miles before really starting to climb and it did occur to me that the stages could have been arranged to end at Howgill (where there was B&B accommodation attached to the campsite) and at Lofthouse or even Ramsgill. Then we should have been fresher for the more strenuous part of the walk and more able to revel in the exhilaration of the wind and the magnificent scenery.

Today we had a stiff climb up to Carlton Moor and then a steep descent into West Burton. As we came down past the chimney of the former lead smelt we saw a farmer busily shearing his sheep next to a caravan which was stacked full of fleeces. He looked lonely and, in any case, the noise of the tractor engine which was powering his shears would have drowned any conversation. I was reminded of a book I had see in Ashbourne before we set out.

The writer was lamenting the demise of the comradeship there used to be among farm workers. He commented that machines have reduced the labour force on farms but have not removed the drudgery.

Farmers are now protected from the elements in their little windowed cabins but they no longer have contact either with other workers or with the land itself.

The pub on the village green at West Burton allows non-customers to use its toilets on payment of 20 pence to children's leukaemia research. The shop is another friendly place but closes for lunch until two o'clock. We decided to forego the opportunity of getting lost in the fields and followed the road along the Walden Beck within sound of the water-fall. The walls were festooned with Yellow Corydalis and Ivy-leaved Toadflax.

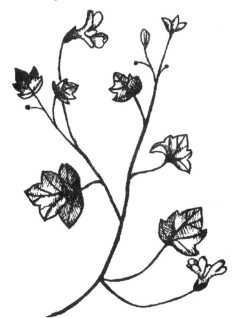

IVY-LEAVED TOADFLAX climbs over walls and has lilac flowers that look like tiny Snapdragons.

As we left West Burton we were talking about the two aspects of repentance: a negative turning from sin and a positive turning to God, trusting Him for forgiveness. By the time we reached Aysgarth our conversation had turned to the Yorkshire cricketers who had played for England.

I didn't count the steps down from the church to the river but there must be about two hundred. As soon as we had arrived at the bottom we were politely invited to climb some more to visit a carriage collection. Instead, we crossed the bridge towards the spectacular Falls. I was pleased to see that the hole in the wall where you can leave your fifty pence is called an Honesty Box. I remembered seeing them on the trolley buses in Huddersfield when I was a child.

All sorts of flowers were growing at the side of the path but the farmer had carefully rooted out all the poisonous Ragwort and stacked it up in tidy piles. No doubt he was aware of the Weeds Act of 1959, which the Government, for some reason, is now wanting to repeal. I should like to see it more rigidly enforced, especially when we have to walk through thistles (also classified as 'injurious').

We soon reached the dismantled Wensleydale Railway. It was frustrating to have to walk alongside and around it but hardly ever on it. Later the same day, however, I was encouraged to learn that the railway-loving public is being invited to buy 'Track Units' at £15 each so that this line can be re-opened, initially from Northallerton to Redmire, but then in sections along Wensleydale. It is hoped one day that trains will be again be running all the way to Garsdale to join the Settle & Carlisle Railway line.

As we approached Askrigg the stiles seemed to become narrower every time we came to one and we could hear the church clock chiming five o'clock. We were allowed nonetheless into the B&B opposite the church for a delicious tea, carefully served by Brian and Thomas, whose mum was standing in for the owners for an hour or two.

The public conveniences are in the Village Hall. I heard a lady commenting to her daughters,

"Aren't they trusting round here! Did you hear the man in Ripon car park? He'd left his keys in the boot of his car and when he came back they were still there!"

The path from Askrigg led through fields and farmland and then along a lovely, unfenced green track. The worst bits were the areas around the gates where the cattle trample through four times a day and especially those parts of the farmyards whichwhich have been concreted. There is no way for the mud and slurry to drain away so it remains inches thick on the surface. I find the old-fashioned cobblestones much better for my boots.

An old farmer was standing in his doorway for a breath of evening air. He asked us about our walk.

"I'd be running it if I were eighteen," he commented.

"So would I!" replied David.

Below Sedbusk the path comes down into Hawes through a field where a sign warned us of a bull. I was wanting a rest so we sat at the top of the field and surveyed its inhabitants. They were mostly sheep and lambs with a couple of calves but then a very long, dark shape made its way across the field towards the path and started to graze just where we were going to have to pass. We decided to pray, and not just for the meeting which was taking place back at home at Little Hill. Down we went, I keeping very close behind my husband, until we were near enough to see that the enormous beast was only a cow! Our prayers had been answered very quickly.

At Hawes Station (now a National Park Centre) we turned left past Outhwaite the Rope-maker's and soon found ourselves at East Burn. We thought we had done well, for it was not even nine o'clock. Mrs. Fothergill, however, obviously considered we were snails in comparison with the two Pennine Way walkers she had found on her doorstep at half past three the previous afternoon.

It was fascinating to hear how her husband and son are both employed at the Wensleydale Creamery. Although it closed down last year it was re-opened just in time for Christmas 1992 and half the former workforce now have their jobs back. It was Mr. Fothergill's great-grandfather, Kit Calvert, bookseller and farmer, who kept the Creamery open when it was threatened with closure in 1935.

There are even plans now to open a Visitors' Centre so that we shall be able to see how the delicious Wensleydale Cheese is made.

A delicious tea carefully served by Brian and Thomas

"I'd be running it if I were eighteen!"

Friday 30th July – Hawes

We like Hawes.

Dick and Sue, with whom we breakfasted, were spending a week there, walking off in different directions everyday. We only spent half an hour in the town centre before following a field path to Appersett. On the way out I bought a car sponge from the ironmongers next to Elijah Allen's Café and the gentleman there cut it for me, with a huge pair of scissors, into two strips to pad the straps of my rucksack.

At Appersett we left the road again. (On the other side of Hawes are Burtersett and Countersett. I sometimes amuse myself by inventing similar sounding village names for every consonant in the alphabet.) After struggling across two stiles, two fields and a couple of bogs, I noticed that we could have followed the road for another few yards to the bridge and come down some steps to join the path along the River Ure. Was this the first step in our growing awareness that roads do at times have advantages over field paths?

The grass was dry but the ground was soggy in places, all the more so when we left the woods and the hay fields and began to climb up to the moors. Even though I am convinced that the government's road-building programme needs to be curtailed, I am still grateful that we do not often have to drive along tracks as stony or as swampy as the one we were following.

Lady Anne Clifford used to ride up here, however. In 1643 this little lady inherited castles at Appleby, Barden Tower, Brough, Brougham, Pendragon and

Skipton and set to work restoring them. In her sixties, seventies and even into her eighties, she was constantly travelling from one of these places to another, supervising the work. Now we were walking on the route she often used, and an old Roman road which dates even further back, to the Bronze Age.

> I began to sing to myself:
> *"When the road is rough and steep*
> *turn your eyes upon Jesus:*
> *He alone has power to keep..."*

Yes, I thought, politicians don't have any real power. All human beings grow old and frail.

> *"Jesus is....*
> *...One on whom you can depend".*

Even my beloved husband had left me way behind. I sat down on a stile and looked back at Addleborough, the hill we had walked past yesterday. What a long way we had come already!

But there was still a long way to go and David had already disappeared up the hill, so I carried on after him. At least, I knew that he would wait for me. That's what marriage is all about: we do things together. Over twenty-six years he has been teaching me that marriage is all about sharing. We are no longer two individuals. Way back at the beginning of time, when God made the first man and the first woman, He ordained that the man should be united with his wife and they become one.

Things haven't changed. That is still the recipe for a successful marriage. Some people suggest that a happily married couple can lead two completely separate lives and indeed there is a sense in which we cannot be constantly holding hands. But where we do have separate interests we talk to each other about them, so that I for instance listen to what David tells me about rocks or railways while he tries to appreciate what I do in the garden or the kitchen. In other aspects of our lives, such as bringing up our daughters or on walking holidays or in the church, we work together.

So here we were, walking up Lady Anne's High Way together. What a beautiful place it was! I had never imagined that there would be such an expanse of pastureland up here where the sheep, still suckling their fast-growing lambs, were enjoying the lazy summer days. In places there were streams crossing the path and I wondered how Lady Anne's carriage had negotiated the boggy bits. Did she ever have to get out and push?

I mentioned Lady Anne to the one walker we met all afternoon. He looked at me rather strangely and said,

"Well, you learn something new every day!" He was obviously not on the A.P.W., just doing a circular walk around the Mallerstang Valley.

What a fantastic view we had! We could see at least one of the Three Peaks: Whernside and, much nearer, Dandrymire Viaduct, with the Coal Road behind it, leading from Garsdale Station to Dent. Looking further north, we could see the Moorcock Inn, Lunds Viaduct and Grisedale Cottages with the footbridge we had crossed on a previous walk.

A sheep was wandering nonchantly along ahead of us, Its lamb saw us coming and called urgently to its mother. I was reminded of the way that A.A. Milne's

> *"James James*
> *Morrison Morrison*
> *Weatherby George Dupree*
> *Took great*
> *Care of his Mother*
> *Though he was only three."*

I tried to say the poem all the way through but I couldn't remember all the words.

While we were eating our lunch we watched a train go past on the Leeds, Settle and Carlisle line.

Later on we passed Lunds Chapel and, further on still, Aisgill where we had once stood on the bridge looking for the now demolished signal box. Elijah Allen's sandwiches had given David extra energy. He set off at such a pace I thought he must be trying to race the next train up 'the long drag'.

We could see the cairns on Wild Boar Fell, up to which we had once climbed with our daughter Ruth. They looked minute from this side of Mallerstang Valley. We crossed the bridge over the infant River Ure and were at the watershed of England because the next stream was the infant Eden. Our view over Upper Wensleydale had changed and now we were looking down towards the Eden Valley. The High Way was coming down now towards Mallerstang Common and the sun was shining in a clear blue sky.

The Thrang Country Hotel came into view and we felt that a cup of tea would crown our afternoon to perfection. When we came closer, however, we could see a sign saying "Tea Room Closed". What a disappointment! But then we saw a smaller sign in the window saying,

"Walkers and Cyclists,
"When we are closed, ring the bell.
We will open if we can."

So we went to the door and were warmly invited inside by Dr. and Mrs. Hamilton. (His book on 'Mallerstang - The Magic Valley' is to be published shortly by Cerberus.) They explained that although the remaining six or so miles to Kirkby Stephen would be nothing to car drivers, it is a long way if you are on foot and feeling thirsty. The Coach House Tea Room was full of interesting information about the area, the Clifford family and other people who had lived there, such as John Knewstubb who was not allowed to become Master of St. John's College, Cambridge, because of his Calvinist views.

We walked along the B6259 as far as Pendragon Castle which may have been built by King Arthur's father, Uther Pendragon. Although Lady Anne restored it in 1660 it is now in a sad state of disrepair.

It had been good to walk along a road where normally we travel too fast to see things properly but now we left it and followed a "green road" to another ruined castle at Lammerside.

Along the way we met a large lamb which had stuck its head through some wire netting and

The lamb ran off without stopping to say "Thank You!".

was stuggling to free itself. It had probably not realised that its horns were growing too long for it to be able to do such things safely. David climbed up on to the bank and managed to force first one horn and then the other back through the fence, at which the lamb ran off without stopping to say "Thank You". David then had to scramble back down off the bank and a couple in a passing car looked quite horrified to see him sitting there, wondering which was the best way to go about it.

Our delightful route down into Kirkby (pronounced Kirby) Stephen finally took us past Wharton Hall, fourteenth century home of the Wharton family. In his will, Philip, Lord Wharton, who died in 1696 at the ripe old age of 83, requested that some of his estate should be used for the free distribution of Bibles, I remember, as a child, learning off by heart several passages of Scripture so that I could receive a "Lord Wharton Bible".

We took a short cut, omitting the Stenkrith Valley which we had visited last year with its unusual holes in the rocks. We crossed the disused Stainmoor Line (Barnard Castle to Tebay) and thought back over the wonderful walk we had just enjoyed. This had probably been the best stage of the whole A.P.W..

We recalled previous walks. The highlight of the Coast to Coast had been climbing up to Nine standards Rigg, whose cairns we had glimpsed a short while ago. What about the Pennine Way?...Our favourite memory of that is HighCup Nick and we should be very near there tomorrow evening. Strange how all the very best bits seem to be in this one area. But, as Phil Crowston said when he welcomed us into their home for the night, "Kirkby Stephen is the centre of the universe!"

P.S. Even at the centre of the universe, fish and chip shops have been known to close at 8 pm. So Be warned

Elaine Crowston, laughing at me in my raincape suggested that this book should be entitled *The Great Big Yellow Snail*, which David later modified to *A Snail on The Trail.*

The flowers are BLUE MEADOW CRANE'S-BILL which we noticed all the way along the walk.

Saturday 31st July – Kirkby Stephen

If yesterday evening we had felt as though we were 'coming home' to Kirkby Stephen, we felt this morning that we were honoured guests. There was even marmite on the table and beautiful creamy porridge. We were able to digest it while our washing was in the launderette (which had been closed when we arrived last night but usually stays open until 9p.m.). We visited The Bookshop and the Tourist Information Centre to find out more about Lady Anne Clifford, the Outdoor Shop where Peter Denby had first told us about the A.P.W., and the baker's next door for packed lunches. These were excellent but they were packed into huge cake boxes. How were we to carry them? David managed to squash his into his rucksack and I tied mine on top of my pack so that I looked like a camel with two humps.

It was drizzling and the clouds were down on the top of the hills. We felt sorry for the couple we had met in the laundrette who were setting off up Nine Standards on the Coast to Coast Walk, especially remembering the wonderful view we had had from the top last year. We therefore decided, especially as David's ankle had been troubling him the previous evening, to stick to the roads for the first part of today's walk.

There was a profusion of flowers along the verges including many that we had seen on the Coast to Coast: Herb Robert, Tufted Vetch, Great Burnet, Bird's-foot-trefoil, Harebells, Black Knapweed, Silverweed Blue Meadow Crane's-bill and masses of Meadowsweet. There were also flowers that I have only learnt to recognise during this holiday, such as

The WILD STRAWBERRY is related to the wild Rose.
It has white flowers with five petals and when its tiny
berries are ripe, they taste beautifully sweet.

clover – coloured Betony, purple Woundwort and two yellow flowers, Nipplewort and Hop Trefoil. We even found some wild strawberries growing all along one stretch of the road.

Everywhere there were the tiny white flowers with four petals of which I had seen examples all the way from Holme in the West Riding. There it had been only a few inches tall and on the hills near Scammonden it was even smaller. Now I realised that there was a great similarity between these small plants and the tall Goosegrass or Cleavers, which clings to other plants and trails over hedges. I had never before noticed its tiny white flowers, even though I have weeded it out of my own garden. I discovered that Goosegrass is a type of Bedstraw. What I had see on the moors was no doubt Heath Bedstraw and maybe some I had seen elsewhere were Woodruff, which is scented.

The trouble is that you can't spend very long smelling wild flowers when your husband is in a hurry. Another reason for our sticking to the road was that we wanted to stay near the Settle - Carlisle line because "Sir Nigel Gresley" was due on the line that afternoon. We had been interested to learn that a dozen drivers and firemen had volunteered earlier this year to retrain in order to man the steam loco-motives which are running every Saturday during the summer.

It is surprising how quickly ankles can heal when you want to see a steam train. David was so far ahead of me that he disappeared out of sight and I began to wonder whether I should see him again before Dufton. But it was only because his watch

Other train-spotters kept arriving until there were fifteen of us on the bridge.

75

was wrong: we ended up at a good vantage point with twenty minutes to wait. As we started on our packed lunches other train spotters kept arriving until there were fifteen of us on that little bridge.

At last we could make out a plume of smoke which came nearer and nearer until the train appeared, hurtling along the track towards us. We could make out its streamlined casing in the blue livery of the late L.N.E.R.

And then it was gone, under the bridge and away down the line towards Kirkby Stephen, getting up speed ready for "the long drag" up to Aisgill Summit. I carried on eating my lunch while the men around me carried on talking about the experience.

"What a lick she was doing!"

"It's not my favourite engine. I prefer 'Princess Margaret Rose'."

"There seemed to be something wrong with one of the valves."

"The change in the timetable will've caught a lot of people out. The train doesn't normally arrive until an hour later than this."

That must have been what Andy was thinking as he drove past and saw us still grouped there, so he kindly stopped and walked back to tell us that the train had already gone. We were interested to learn that he had graduated from the same college as my grandfather (although nearly a century later) and that his wife had decided to give up her part-time teaching job to devote herself to bringing up their family. We were glad to find out that we were all Christians.

"See you again," said Carol "up there".

We came through fields to Great Ormside, a very tidy village with at least two seventeenth century farmhouses. The mint was growing in barrels to keep it from spreading and even the hens had been trained not to squawk. This really was a Railway Afternoon. As well as two sprinters which passed us along the Leeds - Settle - Carlisle line, we saw a double-headed diesel express pulling about a dozen coaches.

It took the "riverside walk" a long time to get us to the Eden. The path seemed to finish and we thought we were being directed through fields again but we were wrong and had to struggle back over a barbed wire fence. Eventually, however, we found ourselves in delightful woodland walking alongside the river. I found a type of St. John's Wort called Tutsan (from the French "tout sain", so called because of its healing properties).

In retrospect, we felt that we could have reached the shopping centre of Appleby more quickly by going left round the castle (now a conservation centre) than by turning right. Still, we were just in time to get a good tea at "The Coffee Pot" before continuing our journey up to Dufton.

Sunday 1st August – Dufton

I lay in bed, basking in the luxury of not having to get up as early as the other guests, who were making an early start along the original Pennine Way. I was still feeling clean from my hot bath the night before but at length made my way down for Mrs. Hullock's excellent breakfast in the old kitchen at Ghyll View, with its spotless range and shining brass pans and copper kettles.

We were having another Rest Day, catching up on correspondence and walking along to the afternoon service at Espland Hill Methodist Church. The sun was shining as we walked back along the road between Honeysuckle and Lady's Bedstraw. David began to whistle:

"Heaven above is softer blue,
Earth around is sweeter green..."

It was from the last hymn we had sung in the service.

"Something lives in every hue
Christless eyes have never seen".

Is it true? I wondered. Do I really appreciate nature more than people who are not Christians? Not necessarily; certainly there are many people who know far more about it than I do. On the other hand, I know for sure that this world did not evolve but was made by a powerful Creator Who is also personal and Who is even interested in me.

I remembered the voices resounding in that little chapel:

"Flowers with deeper beauties shine
Since I know, as now I know,
I am His and He is mine."

We could see the mountains of the Lake District

*HONEYSUCKLE's sweet-scented flowers are
sometimes yellow and sometimes deep pink.
They are followed by clear, dark crimson berries.*

over to the West: Wild Boar Fell over-looking Mallerstang, where we had walked across from the Yorkshire Dales two days previously; Cross Fell, the highest mountain in the Pennines, and the area David Bellamy calls "England's last wilderness" which we should be entering tomorrow: all these wonderful places overlook the Eden Valley.

In such a beautiful area it is easy to praise God but I'm glad that He is also there when things are hard or even just humdrum. In fact, C.S. Lewis suggested that we glorify God more by praising Him during difficult times. I must keep that in mind when we start climbing those mountains tomorrow!

Meanwhile, Mrs. Hullock's evening meal smelt good...

Monday 2nd August – Dufton.

The surgeon and his wife left an hour and a half earlier, the headmaster and his son half an hour before we snails managed to drag ourselves away from Ghyll View, leaving Mr. and Mrs. Hullock with only Snip the dog for company. Having set off so late, we decided that instead of dawdling along field paths with gates and stiles, we would stick to the road up through Knock to Great Dun Fell.

It was drizzling but the forecast was for a brighter afternoon. I noticed some wild Pansies on the bank; the only other ones that I had ever seen were in Teesdale above High Force, not many miles from here as the crow flies. Higher up the road there were Daisies and the even smaller Eye-bright winking up at me along the roadside. With the stream gurgling alongside, this must be a delightful place to be walking on a day such as last Friday, when from Lady Anne's Highway we had been able to see the sunshine illuminating the radar station on Great Dun Fell and making it sparkle with brilliant whiteness.

This morning it was somewhere invisibly above us, hidden in the mist. We looked back and the clouds had lifted just enough for us to see the Eden valley below us. It looked as though the sun was shining but that was probably just a trick of the light, from the gloom of our vantage point. I wondered whether our sheets were out blowing on Mrs. Hullock's clothes line.

We almost caught up with the other two A.P.W. walkers as we were entering the Moor House National Nature reserve. Their shadowy figures

HEARTSEASE or WILD PANSY
has two purple petals and three yellow ones.
When the seed-vessels ripen they split into three sections
with a row of tiny seeds in each.

appeared and disappeared as the visibility came and went, Although it was further by road, we must have saved a lot of time by avoiding the field paths. No sooner had we sat down at the point where the A.P.W. crosses the Pennine Way than two figures loomed out of the mist. It was the couple on the Pennine Way who had left so long before we had. Their more arduous route had included the ascent of Knock Fell.

"Isn't this much more exciting", David greeted them, "than sitting on a Mediterranean beach?"

"I had been thinking that myself," replied Mary, "but now I'm not so sure. My crisps have been blowing out of the bag before I could eat them!"

They walked on and I tried my own packet of crisps. I had nearly finished it when the whole bag blew out of my frozen fingers and across the moor before I had realised what was happening. So just in case you come across a crisp packet on Great Dun Fell, I publicly admit my guilt. Soon afterwards I caught sight of something else in the heather. Was it a scientific instrument for measuring changes in the biosphere? No, it was a sheep, newly shorn and therefore a brilliant white under its blue markings.

We turned off the tarmac road shortly before the radar station. The clouds were lifting and we could see the huge white sphere towering above us. It watched us all the way down the valley. Sometimes it was a luminous white, sometimes darkly silhouetted against the light.

It was still very cold but that was hardly surprising since at 2,500 feet this was the highest point on the A.P.W.. The path was easy to follow, a welcome change from when we had done this section of thePennine Way in thick mist two years ago. We looked up to the top of Cross Fell and wondered whether our friends up there could see very far. When we stopped for lunch in the heather, a few big drops of rain started to fall so I took the opportunity to get out my raincape to protect both me and my rucksack. Even within its yellow walls my hands still took another hour to thaw out properly. And this was August!

There were four sheep on the path ahead of us. I heard a 'plop' and realised that one of them had decided to ford Trout Beck, whereas the other three were perched on the rocks, wondering whether or not to risk getting wet. As David had remarked to me when I was faced with a boggy stretch a little while earlier, "He who hesitates..." Then suddenly a frog jumped out across my path from somewhere near my left elbow. I shrieked (naturally!); the sheep scuttled across the stream in terror and didn't stop running until they were half a mile away from us.

Trout Beck joined the River Tees and flowed away to the South East towards Cow Green Reservoir, after we had passed Moor House, headquarters of the Nature Reserve, where research is taking place into the formation and erosion of peat. A short time later, David said to me. "Do you know the name of this little ditch to our left? Its the South Tyne!"

We were at Tyne Head and making our way very gradually down towards Garrigill. Still, it did not seen quite as tedious as when we had come down

Each red CLOVER flower head actually consists of
many individual flowers,
each shaped like those of a Pea plant.

from Cross Fell two years ago. On the way we noticed the deepest ruby-red Clover I have ever seen.

The sun was shining warmly as we came into Garrigill and the village green looked so attractive that we sat and wrote postcards for half an hour before introducing ourselves to Mrs. Bramwell at the Post Office. The head master and his son arrived after we did because they had faithfully followed the route in the book whereas we had missed out the meanders.

Later that evening we met up again with our friends who were on the Pennine Way and another couple doing the same walk but who were camping. Our conversation centred on the low temperatures that day. Then it turned out that we all had daughters awaiting A-level results. It is only when their children are old enough to be left in the house on their own, that couples like ourselves can come away on these muddy, windswept, walking "holidays". But do we ever grow old enough to be independent?

"We'll have to go to 'phone our elder daughter," said Mary. "She made me promise to let her know each evening that we had made it safely to our destination. She's worried about us!"

Tuesday 3rd August – Garrigill.

Over breakfast we met Rowena and Edwin who, with their parents, were spending a week in Garrigill. Their father had first come when he was doing the Pennine Way eighteen years ago and he liked the place so much that he was now back for his fifth visit.

Because Garrigill is not actually on the A.P.W., we missed out Ashgill and took the road, its verges carpeted with wild flowers such as Selfheal and Mare's-tail. It led to Nenthead, which claims to be the highest village in England, as well as the coldest. Along the way we were wondering whether the couple from Sheffield had made it to Alston to buy an elastic bandage for the lady's twisted ankle.

In Nenthead we took advantage of the existence of a Post Office set up in 1850 by the Quaker-run London Lead Company and also of the toilets which may have some connection with the Public Wash House, also provided for the lead miners.

After leaving Nenthead we finally abandoned tarmac roads to cross open moorland. Of course, it is possible to reach Allendale by road but we had come to walk on the Pennines after all and we were already nearly at their northern limit so we felt that we really ought to make the best of it. It is rather a pity, though, that these moors which look so brown and dry in the distance are really very green and soggy when you actually walk over them. It still surprises me that the higher up you go, the soggier they become but I am assured that this is because of peat's properties of absorbing and retaining water.

The route took us up round The Dodd where we crossed from Westmorland into Northumberland and got our feet wet in the process. At just over two thousand feet, The Dodd is officially a mountain so it was quite cold for the time of the year. It was raining too, by now, but we plodded on for about three miles, clambering down into peat troughs and up out of them again. There was not really any heather but there was moss and weed growing in between the grass.

David was following the map and I was following David. Really it is much easier that way. I have no need to worry further ahead than the next step. I am so glad that I have never been in the habit of reading "horror-scopes" (the spelling is borrowed). I prefer to trust God Who, I know, is working every-thing out for my ultimate good and who does not always choose to tell me what difficulties lie ahead.

I have come to the conclusion that when walking it is best to have a break every hour or so but what would have been the point of sitting on open moor-land in the wind and rain? As we continued down Middle Rigg, however, the rain gradually stopped and the wind soon dried us out so at last we were able to sit down for lunch. The sun came out and we could see farms across the valley on the other side of the infant River West Allen. I watched a little white tanker slowly climbing the hill. Then a tiny white dot of a car appeared, following the lorry, catching up with it and finally overtaking it. We should be joining that road ourselves before very long.

We carried on down the Rigg. Unfortunately our map does not show dry stone walls so after some time we found ourselves in a corner between two of them, with no way out except to go back a very long way. The only thing to do was to climb over. David found a place where there was no barbed wire, left his rucksack and map with me for safe-keeping and climbed over. I passed his pack and mine over to him, took off my cape (which would otherwise have blown over my head and immobilised me) and soon I was sitting astride the wall.

It was further down to the ground on the other side and it took me a very long time but in the end I was over without the wall having collapsed on top of me. We had to perform a similar feat when we came right down the valley to the footbridge across the river and found ourselves on the wrong side of the barbed wire fence, except that this time we went underneath.

The fields on the opposite side seemed to be on a gradient of at least 45° and by the time we reached Spartywell, we both felt in need of rest and refreshment. We sat down for a drink of water and were soon asleep. A couple walked past with two dogs. I opened one eye and the lady said,

"We're walking quietly so as not to disturb you!"

We walked up a track to another stretch of open moor but this part seemed to be quite dry underfoot. We headed for a way-marker post and then looked in vain for another. At last we came to a small cairn and a post that had fallen over. David picked it up and held it back in its hole while I

"Sssh!
Don't wake them!"

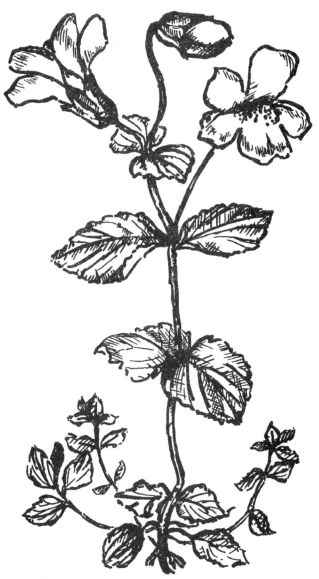

Before we came on this holiday I had never
seen any MONKEY FLOWERS.
They are bright yellow and red and grow in streams.

hammered it in with a stone.

"How do you recognise Elizabeth Gregson?" asked David and then answered his own question: "She's the one whose husband has a flat hand."

I had been wrong about this section of moorland. It may be called Dryburn but it gets wetter underfoot the higher you go. Soon, however, we came to the road. We had discovered that Crowberry Hall was somewhere to our right so we stayed on theroad even when we came to the two chimneys where the A.P.W. route branches off to follow the course of the old mill flues down into Allendale Town. These two flues were used to bring noxious fumes from the Allen Mills up to the top of the moors and at the same time allowed sublimated lead to condense on the brick walls so that it could be recuperated.

Eventually we came over into the valley of the River East Allen and turned right in the direction of Sinderhope. There were pink flowers (Foxgloves, Clover, Willowherb, Knapweed, Spear Thistles and a small clump of Ragged Robin); yellow flowers (the pretty little Tormentil and its taller five-petalled look-alike Wood Avens, as well as the only Monkeyflowers I have ever seen outside the Derbyshire Dales); white flowers (Oxeye Daisy, Blackberry, Hogweed, Stitchwort); and even a few blueflowers (Tufted Vetch and Harebells). Obviously, it must have been a long road! We even found a few wild Raspberries but these were mostly across the ditch out of my reach as we walked by. I was glad that the wind was blowing towards us, bringing the scent of the Meadowsweet and Sweet Cicely, which kept us going as we made our way to Crowberry Hall.

The journey had been worthwhile. Mr. and Mrs. Wentzel are walkers themselves and know what is needed after a long day spent in the open: boots to be dried, socks to be washed, a hot bath, an excellent meal and a bedtime drink. It was an added bonus that they are both very knowledgeable about wild flowers and were able to answer all my questions.

Wednesday 4th August – Allendale

I was dreaming that I was walking through a swimming pool to Castle Hill when David woke me. He was planning a motorway from Spartywell, where we had fallen asleep yesterday, to Spartylea, a village a little further along the River East Allen from Crowberry Hall. Mrs. Wentzel interrupted our fantasising with a cup of tea and a cup of coffee.

She later gave us a wonderful choice of what to eat for breakfast and also told us the best path to take into Allendale Town.The two of them walk there regularly with Sophie and Sandy, their big dogs. On our way down to the river we came to a newly-mown hay field. A little patch was left uncut and I wondered whether it was a miniature Nature Reserve. "No," said David, "it's a roundabout on the Spartylea by-pass".

We stopped in Allendale to buy sandwiches at the Tea Rooms. A group of ladies were having morning coffee and we could tell from their accent that we were now in the North East. They were discussing holiday currency.

"And when you get to Japan, it's serious, man!"

As I had chosen prunes and apricots rather than fresh grapefruit for breakfast, I was still worried about the midges in Kielder Forest. (If you don't understand that last sentence, turn back to the illustration on page 52) I therefore called at the Pharmacy for oil of citronella to protect me. Next I had some difficulty in finding a letter box but as we eventually left Allendale Town, we saw three in quick succession, emblazoned respectively "E VI1 R", "E 11 R" and "G VI R". Then at Keenley

"It's serious, man!"

we saw "VR" and further on still "GR" which I suppose means George V. We had decided to stick to
the roads today, apart from the two miles
intoAllendale from Crowberry Hall. We had had a
hard day yesterday and did not want to get our feet
wet again.

Besides, we have discovered that we can walk
much faster on roads, and David a lot faster than I
can, so that on our way up to Whitfield from
Whitfield Hall, he was soon far ahead of me. I was
just feeling glad that at least I was carrying the
sandwiches, when he called out from behind me! He
had been hiding behind a wall in the churchyard
and we decided that this would be the best place to
have lunch, as the road was narrow and the hedges
were high.

It was not long however before the road was going
over the moor. We were looking west towards the
very end of the Pennines, whilst to our left was West
Allendale and the high ground we had crossed yesterday. Then we turned north towards Hadrian's
Wall and the Cheviots.

Suddenly we realised that we were coming down
towards an opencast coal mine. There were lorries
like little matchbox toys beneath us and an enormous slag heap to our left. I felt quite upset at this
blot on the landscape.

The nearer we came, however, the more we appreciated the efforts that are being made to camouflage
the damage to the environment. Grass is beginning
to grow over the slag heap and where the road has
had to be re-routed, the verges have been re-seeded.

The whole area looked tidy and hygienic and we later noticed that the pipeline down to Melkridge, along with the enormous coal hopper beside the railway line, have been painted a discreet olive green. Really, we were quite glad to see that coal is still being mined at least somewhere in Britain. The whole project had been invisible until we turned on to Plenmeller Common and would also be, no doubt, from down in Haltwhistle. (It does apparently ruin the view south from Hadrian's Wall but the terrible weather the following day distracted our thoughts from such things.)

As we came further down we could see the town nestling in the Tyne Gap where the River South Tyne turns to run east to Hexham. We could see a sprinter on the Carlisle - Newcastle railway line, traffic on the A69 and cars higher up behind the town on the Military Road. We could even make out some of the crags where Hadrians Wall runs along the Whin Sill.

We came down through farmland to Plenmeller and passed the factory where Cascelloid plastic squeezy bottles are made. We were glad to be allowed to cross the Tyne by the old bridge to the station, since cars now have to travel further along to a new road bridge. We walked along Westgate and suddenly found that Hall Meadows was just across the road: a most attractive house in a beautiful garden.

After a lovely hot bath we went out to find something to eat. As we were waiting for our pizzas to cook, a little girl called Katie came in to buy a bag of chips while her mother waited outside in the car. I wondered why Katie was standing on the low windowsill, until I realised that it was so that she could actually see the lady behind the counter.

Earlier that afternoon I had been thinking back to information I still remember from the I-SPY books that used to be published by the now defunct *News Chronicle*. As we wandered back along Main Street, what should we see in a shop window but a display of I-SPY books! (now published by Michelin).

Back at Hall Meadows, Mrs. Humes told us that she has had well over a dozen people so far this year trying out the Alternative Pennine Way. Apparently most of them have made it to the end!

"I've got a pound coin!"
said Katie.

Thursday 5th August – Haltwhistle

I woke to hear the rain pouring down outside. This was the day we had been dreading. We had seventeen and a half miles to walk by 5-30 p.m. in order to catch the bus from Falstone (where there is one hotel) to Bellingham (where we had previously enjoyed Mr. and Mrs. Batey's hospitality while walking the Pennine Way).

David had been reading up about the difficulties of finding the way through the conifers that would make up two thirds of today's section of the A.P.W.. I had been warned at least three times about the midges in Kielder Forest and midges always make a lasting impression on me. Now, the fact that it was raining so hard encouraged us to wonder whether there were any other ways of reaching Bellingham. (pronounced "Bellin-jum").

We had ordered an early breakfast and as soon as we came down, Mrs. Humes asked us whether we had thought about getting the bus. Her dining room is as well-stocked as the Tourist Information Centre so she had no difficulty in finding us a schedule of bus times. We were able to work out a completely different route which would involve almost the same walking distance but which would take us directly to Bellingham. This would mean we were not obliged to arrive at any particular time, with the added advantage that we should be walking on wet roads rather than wet muddy paths. Instead of rushing off on our seventeen and a half mile walk, we therefore found ourselves dawdling over the toast, discussing the history of the north of England with a teacher from Wakefield.

We had decided to walk up to the Military Road and catch the first bus to Chollerford. As the bus would not even be leaving Haltwhistle until 11 a.m., we had time to call at the bank on the way, after saying Goodbye to the comfort and cleanliness of Hall Meadows. We climbed up beside Haltwhistle Burn, which is really quite a wide river with some impressive falls, particularly after a night of rain.

The rain had been coming down steadily for several hours at least and did not look as though it had any intention of changing its ways. We were wearing our maximum of protective clothing, including gaiters, but one of the characteristics of water must surely be its ability to seep through anything. We waited for the bus outside the Milecastle Inn, looking across to the remains of one of the mile-castles on Hadrian's Wall, and received sympathising glances from people in passing cars.

We had the bus almost to ourselves and were able to follow the Wall for fourteen miles, passing Housesteads Fort and going right off the road to Vindolanda, in case anyone was waiting at the bus stop there. No one was.

At Chollerford we let the driver go on his way with a completely empty bus while we tried to find the path along the former Border Counties Railway line. As we gingerly descended the slippery stone steps at the side of the bridge, I could smell the aniseed scent of Sweet Cicely, although its flowers had all gone and only the dark brown seed pods were left. An earlier bridge near this point had carried Hadrian's Wall and the Military Road across the

*SWEET CICELY has an aniseed scent
even after the white flowers have fallen.*

River North Tyne.

At Chollerton we took the road which follows the Border Counties Railway line up to Wark (it rhymes with "dark"). We saw signal boxes, embankments, cuttings and a platelayer's hut. In the Barrasford Arms Hotel on the way to the Ladies' Toilet there is a wonderful display of photographs of the Border Counties line. It was opened on 1st. July 1862 and on the same day the Border Counties Railway amalgamated with the North British Railway but the line kept its original name. It ran up to Riccarton Junction where it met the Waverley line and North British engines used to come down from Scotland as far as Hexham. We kept wondering whether it was a cloud we could see in the distance or a puff of smoke, telling us that Wandering Willie or another of the D30 Scott's Class like The Talisman was coming towards us, or even a D49 Hunt class locomotive like The Percy or The Rufford.

When we arrived in Barrasford we heard a lady say to her friend,

"It's blooming awful weather, mind!" but by the time we left it had stopped raining. There was a pedestrian footpath at the side of the road but I could scarcely put my foot down without crushing a snail. I looked to see whether I could find two snails climbing up a Blue Meadow Crane's-bill plant but all I could find were two slugs on some Hogweed.

"Haway, lass, what 'ya deein'?" David called back to me.

"I was looking at a snail," I replied.

"One snail looking at another," came the rejoinder.

*HOGWEED is one of the many hedgerow plants
which have large, white flower-heads.
Like its relative, wild Angelica, its stalks are hollow.*

Haltwhistle – Bellingham

The North Tyne valley is beautifully wooded. The roads were extremely quiet, with about as many heavy lorries (mostly heading for the quarry near Gunnerton) as cars. We passed a lot of Scabious and Burdocks which I first noticed last year in Whitcliffe Woods near Richmond and again this year at Bouthwaite north of Pateley Bridge.

I heard an engine over to my left.

"Is that a train?" I enquired somewhat naïvely.

"There's British Rail for you," answered David. "Thirty-seven years late! No, love, it's not a train. It's an aeroplane,"

Wark Station had been made into a private house but it still had its platform. Nearby, however, some houses had been built right on the line. The signal box was still standing but looking redundant.

There is no tea room in Wark but there are clean public conveniences, a well-stocked Post Office and a garage which advertises "Hot Snacks". It is worth crossing the bridge over the impressively wide River North Tyne just to see this pretty village grouped round an attractive green.

Meadowsweet was scenting the air and Silverweed doing its best to colonise the side of the road as we walked on to Birtley. We had left the Border Counties line for the time being and were on an even smaller road. There was no traffic to drown out the sound of the sheep calling to their lambs and yet there were empty drinks cans lying between the Betony and the Tufted Vetch, along with empty packets of Concentrated Worm Drench. The Honeysuckle was in bloom and the Rowan trees already had red berries in a little plantation half way up the "bank" (which means 'hill' in this part of England). And so we reached Birtley, joint winner of the Northumberland Best Kept Village Award 1989.

I had expected the next part of the day's walk to be rather ordinary but it turned out to be a memorable experience. After the climb up to Birtley we were in a position to overlook a large section of Northumberland. We looked south to the Whin Sill crowned by Hadrian's Wall and our eyes swept round via Kielder Forest (where we were supposed to have been today) to the Cheviots in the north, where we hoped to be in a day or two. Down below us flowed the North Tyne in its well-wooded valley, with the railway line following it (although we could not make it out from where we were).

We were on a gated road and a dog was barking ferociously at the far side of the next gate. We were thankful to find that it was escorted by a gentleman who told us that he lived in "Bortley". He asked us where we were going and told us he often walked to Bellingham along the railway line. This sounded interesting so we followed his instructions to go down to the Heugh Farm (pronounced Hee'-uff), past it and up on to the bridge.

"Torn reet," he had said and so we found ourselves walking on the former Border Counties railway line.

After a while we came to a gate marked 'Private' so we left the line and climbed up again to where we found that we had an excellent view of Redesmouth

Junction. Here the railway bends round to the left towards Bellingham with the River North Tyne, whereas the Wansbeck line branches off to the right towards Morpeth, following the River Rede. Although this used to be such an important junction (and indeed the line from Bellingham to Redesmouth stayed open until 1963), Redesmouth is only a tiny hamlet. It probably increased its population by almost fifty per cent when the station and signal box were converted into homes.

We crossed the Rede on the road bridge built on the footings of the viaduct that once carried trains on the Border Counties line. After that we followed the line all the way into Bellingham. It was a lovely summer's evening and I must admit that I often found myself more interested in the beautiful Scabious growing at the side of the road. Nevertheless, following a line on foot certainly helps one to admire the skill of the Victorian engineers who built it about a hundred and forty years ago.

Even such an idyllic walk has to end and we were glad to leave our packs with Mr. Batey at Lynn View while we went for fish and chips. Our evening ended as a social gathering round the telephone box where various Pennine Way walkers were also waiting to phone home. We could recognise each other by our boots! A group of four lads were walking from Kirk Yetholm to Edale. They were obviously physically capable of finishing the walk but so far they had done little more than to argue and fall out with each other. We wondered whether they would ever reach their destination.

Friday 6th August – Bellingham

We had intended catching the 8.25 a.m. bus to Falstone but once again we changed our plans. "In for a penny, in for a pound": if we could deviate from the official A.P.W. route yesterday and enjoy it so much, we may as well do so again. It would be a lot further to walk to Byrness from Bellingham than from Falstone but Mr. Batey had a video of "The Wanny Line" and he said that we could watch it after breakfast.

When we came downstairs, the other four guests had switched on breakfast-time TV. Ronald Biggs in Rio de Janeiro was saying that he didn't feel any regret about the Great Train Robbery and didn't think he had done anything wrong. I had just been reading what Paul wrote to Timothy: "They shall turn away their ears from the truth".

There was a lady staying at Linn View on her way to meet her sons at Kirk Yetholm and two footballers who were doing the Pennine Way as a sponsored walk for 'Jimmy's'. Their friend was driving a van with all their luggage, so they only had tiny rucksacks to carry.

"They're doing it the easy way," we thought.

The video began with the nostalgic "Song of the Wild Wanny Line":

"Green grows the grass on the railway track
That men brought to life and then flung back".

The Wansbeck Railway was completed by 1865 and linked the North Eastern Railway line at Morpeth with the Border Counties line at Redesmouth Junction. It was mainly a goods line for coal and cattle; the leisurely, infrequent passenger service

108

was withdrawn in 1952 and the line was closed to freight traffic in 1963. What we were watching was a special excursion in 1966 when the 'Wansbeck Piper' travelled from Newcastle to East Woodburn and back. It could not go further on to Redesmouth because that part of the line had already been torn up.

After all the phantom locomotives of the previous day and the trains we had spotted in the distance near Haltwhistle and Haworth and Kirkby Stephen, I really appreciated the excitement and the human element of this National Trust video. This last train to East Woodburn was also the longest ever seen on that line. It had eleven coaches and was a "double-header", being pulled by two locomotives' which were coupled back to back (or tender to tender) so that when they were shunted to the other end of the train, the leading engine was still facing the right way. We were thrilled to see, among the 640 passengers, Jack Armstrong and Pat Jennings playing the Northumbrian pipes, as we had seen them play at Wallington Hall many years ago. The excursion culminated in a visit to the Bellingham Show.

Snails that we are, we finally left Bellingham at 11-30 a.m. but at least the delay had allowed us to digest our enormous breakfast. Leaving so late, we could not even take the Pennine Way path because we have learnt from experience that it is much quicker to walk along minor roads and tracks, so long as they are going in the right direction. After all, A. Wainwright went along roads on his Pennine Journey of 1939 so why shouldn't we?

The roads we were walking on
were not very busy.

On the western horizon we could see the forest and wondered whether we could make out Kielder Water in the misty distance. Nearer at hand, Clover was growing along the verges: a brilliant raspberry-pink colour here. We turned off on a gated road to Sundaysight and caused consternation among the lambs that we passed. Mostly they ran away from us but occasionally one would decide to stand his ground and stare us out. Then, more often than not, at the very last moment he turned tail and fled like the wind.

We came to a cross-roads that seemed vaguely familiar and David reminded me that two years ago, when we were on the Pennine Way, we had seen three cars parked at a cattle grid just up the road. Before we came right up to them, two of the cars had left and then we discovered that the third car had a broken back window. The following day, up on the Cheviots, we had met a large family who were walking the Pennine Way using two cars to ferry their luggage. Apparently it was one of their cars that we had seen and they confirmed our suspicion that we had disturbed the intruders. We were glad to hear that very little had been stolen.

We had now covered six miles in two hours so felt that it must be time for lunch. As we sat in the heather, a cyclist came slowly up the hill. He had driven over from Morpeth to leave his car at Kielder for a day's cycling. Kielder is fast becoming the tourist centre of the North of England. There are guided walks in the forest (from 'easy' to 'strenuous'), deer-stalking expeditions, Land-Rover safaris, visits to sawmills and there is even a ferry on Kielder Water.

The mist was coming nearer and we had only been there for forty minutes before we were starting to feel quite chilly so we walked on towards the forest. We passed a man mending a drystone wall, (the second we had seen that day). In answer to my query he replied,

"Heavy work, aye," in a thick Northumbrian brogue.

We passed a sign saying Gibshiel Forest and saw fire beaters stacked ready for use. So far there were not many trees and the track was very easy to follow. Then after some time we came to the point where the Pennine Way enters the Redesdale Forest, so now we had actually swapped right over from the A.P.W. to the P.W.. The flies swarmed up to greet us, so out came the oil of citronella. A little while later, David turned to me, saying,

"Can you smell the trees? Oh no, it's you! I'll have to make up a song called 'I married a Smelly Tree'."

As we walked, we were reading about God's ways of chastening and disciplining His children because He loves us and wants the best for us. This really seemed to make sense in the context of this holiday. The hard walking and the heavy rucksacks make the rest and sleep so much more welcome. We felt really to have benefited from all the exercise, just as God allows problems to come into our lives so that we can learn from the experience and grow.

We sat down among the Silverweed and the Eyebright for a rest and were thrilled to see, coming down the ride behind us, the couple from Sheffield

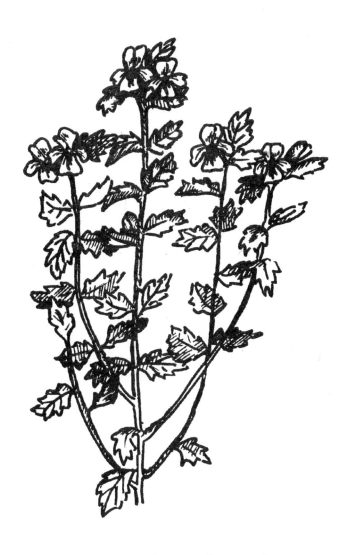

EYEBRIGHT is only a small, insignificant
plant but its tiny white flowers are pretty
when you examine them closely.

who are doing the Pennine Way. The lady (who had twisted her ankle on her way into Garrigill) was now walking quite well. They went on their way ahead of us with all their camping gear.

At Blakehopeburnhaugh there is B&B accommodation and then the Pennine Way forks off left whereas we continued up the Forest Drive. I was surprised to see how many cars were coming downit, presumably to take the toll road to Kielder Castle. We followed the A68 downhill towards the Border Park Café at Byrness (pronounced Burness). A caravan coming up the hill towards us gave us a wide berth, as did the lorry behind it, but the cars following the lorry, perhaps frustrated by their position in the queue, came much closer to the side of the road where we were walking. The closest shave, however, came from a car that came up behind us, completely on the wrong side of the road, intent on overtaking a van that was slowing down to enter the garage 200 yards ahead.

After a good meal, we found a lane which took us through Willowherb and Meadowsweet directly to Mrs. Henderson's house on Otterburn Green. As she had done when we were on the Pennine Way, she welcomed us with a "cup of tea" of the type which requires plates to hold the homemade cake and scotch pancakes.

Saturday 7th August – Byrness

I drew back the curtains and saw a rainbow. Never mind: you know what they say about "Rain before seven...." We were having an early breakfast because it was Mrs. Henderson's birthday and she was going on the Byrness annual children's outing to South Shields. Her great-grand-daughter, who had been staying the night, had already gone home to get ready for the trip.

By just after 7 a.m., Pennine Wayfarers were already setting off on their twenty-seven mile walk to Kirk Yetholm. We only had 19 and a half miles to do to Jedburgh, so we had time to waterproof our boots and to 'phone our daughter (because there would not be any telephone boxes along the way!).

Whereas the Pennine Way route from Byrness begins with a steep, almost vertical, climb through woods and rocks, the A.P.W. makes the same ascent at an angle, up one of the Forest rides, which is much easier. There were even sign-posts, which had been practically non-existent for the previous 250 miles. Even at 8-30 a.m.. the flies were in evidence so I got the oil of citronella out again. Whether it was that or whether it was the steady drizzle I cannot say but I reached the top without being bitten.

David waited for me at the top where we left the road and started to walk across rough grass. Very soon we reached a gate and decided that we really ought to be wearing our gaiters because the grass was so wet, so this became the Gaiter Gate. We were following a path but before long it veered off in the wrong direction, so we had to struggle over tussocky grass to find the right path.

At three minutes to ten we crossed the border into Scotland. After we had walked a quarter of a mile under an imaginary cross of St. Andrew, we realised that we should have turned right at the trig point so we had to walk a quarter of a mile back. (I know because I counted my steps. It was 439 yards to be precise.) There should have been a glorious view over Catcleugh Reservoir from here but we could not see a thing because of the mist.

We stayed just inside Scotland and followed the fence along the top edge of Redesdale Forest. The trees had a very stately look about them and I felt almost as though we were walking in the grounds of a stately mansion, except that we were no longer walking on gravel paths. Far from it! I felt tremendous admiration for the farmers who maintain that Border Fence. It was in excellent condition, despite the fact that the posts are all standing in such soggy ground.

In the places where the fence crosses the wettest bogs it has been strengthened by boards fastened below the wire netting and these were strong enough to take our weight as we inched our way along crabwise. In one place where the strengthened fence crossed a swampy hollow, I decided not to trust it and climbed over to England where the peat was drier. The most succulent bilberries seem to grow in England. It was a strange experience to be standing in Scotland and gathering bilberries in England. I kept wondering what would happen if they moved the fence an inch or two when they were working on it. Would it start a war?

There was not really any point now in trying to walk around the wettest parts. We both had lakes in our boots. To be more accurate, it was like having your feet in warm foot-baths. The only trouble was that if you stood still for a second or two, to consult the map for example, the water quickly went cold.

At least it was not raining now.

"Lifting, lifting," said David as he looked at the clouds, in just the way his father used to say "Testing, testing," into the tape recorder. Even though we could not see the tops of the hills, we could see down into the valley. In fact it almost looked as though the sun was shining over Jedburgh whereas the Border Range to our right was dank and misty. Those Pennine Wayfarers we had seen in Byrness would not be able to see very far.

As we walked along through this deserted wilderness, we suddenly found that over the trees of a small plantation we could see the roofs of Upper Hindhope Farm. We walked downhill past a group of rather inquisitive horses towards Nether Hindhope and there I \saw my first Scottish Harebells, the Bluebells of Bonnie Scotland. I was surprised to find such a little community up here in this remote corner of the Cheviots.

We came to a cross roads and turned left to join Dere Street, once a Roman Road but now a country lane. We had been walking for five hours so we felt that it was time to sample the sandwiches that Mrs.

Henderson had got up at 5 a.m. to make for us. We were hoping that she and her great-grandchildren were enjoying their day in South Shields. The first thing I did, however, was to find some dry socks in my bag, take off my gaiters, boots and wet socks and dry my feet in the fresh air.

We sat there for an hour before walking on, with me exulting in my dry feet. What I had not realised was that Dere Street is not a tarmac road all the way along and in fact very soon it became a grassy path with mud in places. On the other hand, we had wonderful views to our left over the bumpy hills of the Cheviots.

The sheep, which were all white here, suddenly scattered. Someone was coming. Was it a detachment of roman legionnaires? No, it was three teenage sisters, obviously enjoying their holiday in Scotland and followed at a sedate distance by their parents.

After we had been walking for another hour we sat down to admire the sky. We could see dark clouds (especially over the Pennine Way), grey clouds, light clouds and even a bit of blue sky. It had rained again this afternoon but was fine once more by now. There did seem to be a little break in the clouds over South Shields. We wondered whether Mrs. Henderson was enjoying an ice-cream.

My toes were feeling slightly damp. Was it because I had not put my gaiters back on? Was it because my boots had not had time to dry out properly over lunch? Was it an indication that I need to buy some new boots? I started to count up how

Was it a detachment of
Roman soldiers?!

*LADY'S BEDSTRAW has clusters of tiny yellow flowers
and circles of pointed leaves growing round the stem.*

many miles I have walked in this pair. Probably eight hundred, anyway.

It was a lovely afternoon by now. Even David said to me,

"Look at all the wild flowers!" So I proceeded to tell him what they were.

"The big white ones are Yarrow. It grows in our lawn at home. Its other name is Millfoil, meaning a thousand leaves, because of its feathery leaves. The other white flowers are Clover.

"The yellow ones that look like dandelions are actually Cat's-ear. They grow in our front garden too and I remember seeing them on the roadside shortly after we crossed the M62. The spiky yellow flowers are Lady's Bedstraw. We were walking past those last Sunday on our way back to Dufton from Espland Hill".

Dere Street was turning left and becoming a road again. A couple of cars were parked here and, as we approached, one of them drove away. I tried in vain to see its number plate and scrutinised the other car to make sure that its windows were not broken.

The road was downhill and I was able to continue reminiscing.

"Those tiny white stars are Stichwort. There was some growing at Spartywell, where we sat down and fell asleep. Those little yellow flowers are Bird's-foot-Trefoil, which has leaves like clover leaves. There's another flower that looks like it, only it's taller and its leaves are narrower. There's a patch of it here with just a few flowers left on it. It's called Meadow Vetchling. I found that out, somewhere near

Haddon Hall. And this little white flower is Eyebright. It was growing on the slopes of Thorpe Cloud when we were coming down into Dovedale."

"Dovedale," repeated David. "Do you remember Biggindale? And the cup of tea in the summer-house? Doesn't it seem a long time ago! We've come a long way since then."

Dere Street turned back into a path again, with slippery mud in places as it went down to the river. The Romans probably forded Oxnam Water but a footbridge has been built since then so we set off to find it. This in itself was quite an adventure as we pushed our way through giant wild rhubarb leaves and Blue Meadow Crane's-bill. (I still didn't see any snails climbing up it.) We felt like explorers in the jungle and once again I was thankful not to be walking in shorts.

The wooden footbridge was quite modern and firmly set in concrete foundations but the concrete itself had slipped so that the bridge was tipped at a rakish angle. Nevertheless we were able to cross safely and eventually we left Dere Street to walk gradually downhill along a quiet metalled road towards Jedburgh.

Because of the extra miles we had put in on Friday, I should soon have been following David for 275 miles. This morning I had read what Paul says in his second letter to Timothy: "I have finished my course". We had just been looking back on a three week walk. Paul had been looking back over half a lifetime of following the Lord Jesus Christ.

I found some wild raspberries and shared them

with David. Marriage is all about sharing. But Christian marriage also includes following the Lord Jesus Christ together. There is a hymn which says:

"Blindly we stumble when we walk alone
Involved in shadows of a darkening night.
Only with Thee we journey safely on."

I thought back to the walk up to Carlton-in-Coverdale last week. That night had been 'darkening' before we arrived at Middleham House but God had kept us safe, not by some miraculous intervention but simply by helping us to use our map and compass wisely. He has given us a map for our journey through life too. It is called the Bible and we try to base our lives on its teaching.

We could see Jedburgh by now. There was the Abbey, a roofless ruin but still so beautiful. Later on we should see the houses where Mary Queen of Scots and Bonnie Prince Charlie and William and Dorothy Wordsworth had stayed. We came over Dorothy Wordsworth had stayed. We came across Canongate Bridge, the 'Auld Brig' and neither the Sheriff nor the Provost were there to greet us but flowers were smiling at us from every street corner and every window ledge.

We made our way to Craigowen Guest House in High Street.

"Congratulations!" we said to each other.

A Companion Book

by

Elizabeth Gregson

"A Wife on the Walk"

A walk along the 'Coast to Coast' long distance footpath sounds so simple, but what a delightful glimpse of a happy wife and husband twenty-five years marries.

They enjoy God's wonderful land just walking and wondering at the beauty of nature.

Also, with the determination and resolve – as in married life – to see it through together to the end, no matter what might lay ahead

This book is no travelogue or guide, just a wife's view of walking and hand illustrations show what they both saw during this unusual celebration of twenty-five years of marriage

Published December 1992
Paperback 64 pages   Price £2.95

Also by

Elizabeth Gregson

by Winifred Mary Ruston

Illustrated by Ruth Hadfield

Polly and Alice

This unusual book is in two parts. The first, a story for children was written some years ago, by an aunt of Elizabeth Gregson, but never published.

It is in reality an autobiography set in villages in Northamptonshire during the 19th century. The second part, written and compiled by Elizabeth provides a factual background to the story and is a fascinating picture of village life at a time of change from an agricultural to an industrial society.

The book contains unique archive material by way of drawings and photographs – the earliest being 1816.

To anyone with an interest in British social history and those who may want to introduce children to the subject this book is a must.

First published December 1990

Second edition December 1992

Paperback 160 pages   **Price: £3.95**

V·O·L·C·A·N·O
PUBLISHING

For a complete list of our publications
please send S.A.E.

to

Volcano Publishing
13 Little Lunnon,
Dunton Bassett,
Leics. LE17 5JR

Our books should be found
in all good booksellers
but in case of difficulty
please write to the address above.